The Middle Ages

Andrea Bachini

Illustrations by: Alessandro Baldanzi,
Studio Inklink, Studio L.R. Galante

BARRON'S

DoGi

English translation © Copyright 1999
by Barron's Educational Series, Inc.
Original edition © 1999 by DoGi spa, Florence, Italy
Title of original edition: *Il Medioevo*
Italian edition by: Andrea Bachini
Illustrations by: Alessandro Baldanzi; Studio Inklink;
Studio L.R. Galante
Editor: Benedetta Zini
Graphic Design: Sebastiano Ranchetti
Art Director and Page make up: Sebastiano Ranchetti;
Sansai Zappini
English translation by: Paula Boomsliter, for Lexis

All inquiries should be addressed to:
Barron's Educational Series, Inc.
250 Wireless Boulevard
Hauppauge, NY 11788
http://www.barronseduc.com

Library of Congress Catalog Card No.: 99-66722

International Standard Book No. 0-7641-0948-0

Printed in Italy
9 8 7 6 5 4 3 2 1

Table of Contents

4 The West Under Siege
40 Farmers, Knights, and Monks
68 Urban Civilization
92 Empires and Sovereign States
106 Toward World Politics
120 Index

THE WEST UNDER SIEGE

From the fifth through the tenth centuries, when Rome no longer ruled the Mediterranean, massive migrations drastically changed the world. In the Dark Ages, the Byzantine, Muslim, and Chinese civilizations had a higher culture than any Western European people.

The Pax Romana

By the mid-first century B.C., the Romans had conquered all the territory touching the Mediterranean Sea, which they called (with justifiable pride) *mare nostra*. From Britain to Asia Minor, from the shores of the Atlantic Ocean to the Black Sea, Rome's legions had established a single legal system, Roman law, and a single language, Latin, and had made the roads safe for travel and trade. Agriculture and crafts enjoyed the largest single market that had ever existed anywhere.

The art and culture of the Greeks had spread in the fourth century B.C. with Alexander the Great's conquests; Hellenism and Romanism later fused to lend unity to the Mediterranean area. Even though the cultural identity of the Latin-speaking West was

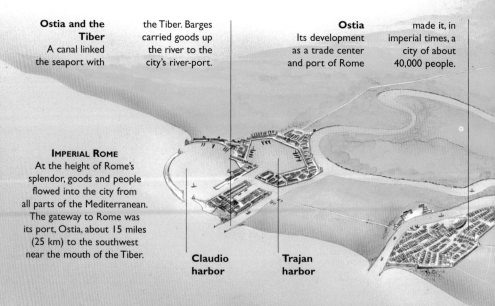

Ostia and the Tiber
A canal linked the seaport with the Tiber. Barges carried goods up the river to the city's river-port.

Ostia
Its development as a trade center and port of Rome made it, in imperial times, a city of about 40,000 people.

IMPERIAL ROME
At the height of Rome's splendor, goods and people flowed into the city from all parts of the Mediterranean. The gateway to Rome was its port, Ostia, about 15 miles (25 km) to the southwest near the mouth of the Tiber.

Claudio harbor

Trajan harbor

most profoundly influenced by Rome, in the lands where Greek was spoken, the Oriental cultural expressions were jealously preserved. In the first century A.D., there began a period of relative peace known as the Pax Romana. And it was at this time that a new religion, Christianity, also began to take hold. Since it proposed equality in a society whose economy has always been based on slavery, it began its spread among the humblest and poorest strata of the population. Despite the Roman tradition of religious tolerance, certain emperors persecuted Christians for political reasons. Then, in the fourth century A.D. Christianity became the official religion of the empire—and as it worked its way up among the higher classes, it became a valuable feature for social unity. Valuable, but insufficient, since by the mid-third century

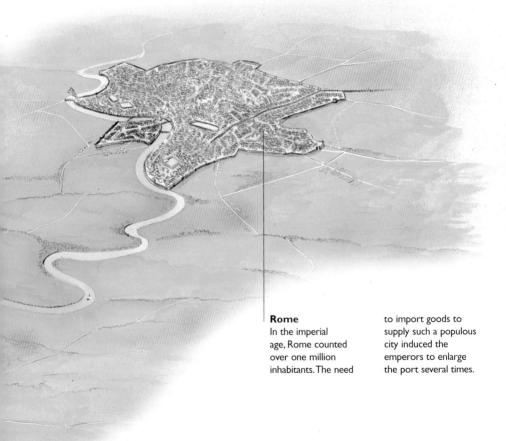

Rome
In the imperial age, Rome counted over one million inhabitants. The need to import goods to supply such a populous city induced the emperors to enlarge the port several times.

THE PORT OF OSTIA
The ships that landed here brought slaves and amber from the Orient, furs from the North, and precious woods and ivory from Africa.

The ships
A medium-sized Roman ship was 60 feet (18 m) long and held 50 tons of cargo. It could contain more than 5,000 gallons of wine in 500 amphoras.

The goods
When ships debarked in the port, goods were loaded onto smaller craft that sailed up the Tiber to Rome.

A.D., Rome was already facing serious difficulties on all frontiers of its enormous territory in Europe, North Africa, and Asia. The failing sense of loyalty to the state and of troop unity, political instability, and economic and financial crisis sealed the fate of Rome.

The pressure exerted by the barbarian populations against Rome's borders increased. "Barbarians," for the Greeks and Romans, were all those peoples who did not speak their languages and whose cultures were different from theirs. Nonetheless, these same barbarians, as they penetrated the territory of the empire, began to play an increasingly active role within the Roman army. Emperor Constantine the Great (r. 312–337) had in the meantime introduced some of the fundamental scenarios of what the world would be like when the single Roman Empire was no more. After having granted freedom of worship to the Christians, he addressed the doctrinal controversies that divided the Western and Eastern churches at the Nicene Council of 325. He also, however, built a new capital, named Constantinople in his honor, on the site of the ancient city of Byzantium on the shores of the Bosphorus, and thus laid the material basis for the future division of East and West. At the social level, a major transformation in agriculture was taking place. Slaves, the majority of the workforce, became harder and harder to come by. In their place, work was done by those who were legally free as tenants but in practice bound, from father to

The main square was enclosed by a portico, with the offices of the merchants and the trade associations: ship outfitters, ropemakers, and grain weighers. Ostia also had storehouses for the grain, oil, and wine not immediately demanded by the Roman market.

son, to the land. After Emperor Theodosius I (r. 379–395), the division of the empire into two parts became a political fact. From then on, the Eastern Empire acted independently. It succeeded in pushing into the western portion many of the invaders, who crossed the imperial frontiers in ever increasing numbers. By the last 30 years of the fifth century, the pressure had become so great as to cause the final collapse of the Western Roman Empire (A.D. 476). But who were these people who had always pushed against Rome's borders?

The Germans

A number of populations of Indo-Europeans, known to the Romans from the time of Caesar (first century B.C.), lived along the northern border of the empire. These were Germanic tribes with similar lifestyles and customs. They farmed land that was the property of the tribal group as a whole. Caesar believed that the custom existed so that the individuals would not become too attached to the land and accumulate excessive wealth. These "semi-nomads," often migrating within tribal territories, preferred cattle- and pig-raising to agriculture.

Among these peoples, in the second–third century A.D., were the Ostrogoths, the Alemanni, the Visigoths, the Saxons, the Angles, the Bavarians, and the Franks. Their cultural traditions were oral, and their religions still primitive: they worshiped the heavenly bodies and ven-

The Valkyries were demigods, guardian angels of sorts, who descend on horseback to the battlefield to hasten the heroes to victory or, in case of defeat, to conduct them to Valhalla, as the god Odin willed.

A GERMANIC MYTH
The myth of Siegfried slaying the dragon was set to paper in the 13th century, but it is inspired by Old Norse oral tradition. The gold of the Rhine, stolen from the Nibelungen, is guarded by the dragon. Prince Siegfried slays the dragon and recovers the treasure.

The Nibelungen were subterranean creatures, metalworkers, and the custodians of treasures.

The dragon was originally a giant, creatures that in Nordic mythology were gods of evil.

Siegfried, the hero of unequaled force and beauty, slays the dragon to recover the gold of the Nibelungen.

The treasure was stolen by the giants from the Nibelungen.

THE GERMANIC, SLAVIC, AND HUNGARIAN INVASIONS
Pushed westward by Asian nomadic populations, Germanic peoples (4th–6th centuries), and later Slavs (9th century), settled within the territory covered by the Roman Empire.

The Germans of the coasts and of the steppes
The first were the Saxons, Frisians, and Danes. The latter were the Goths, located near the Baltic Sea and the lower course of the Danube since the third century.

Britain
The Romans left Britain in 407. In the mid-5th century, it was occupied by Jutland Danes, Angles, and Saxons, who created a dozen or more kingdoms.

The Franks
unified the territories of Gaul and, starting in the 6th century under king Clovis I, expanded from the Rhine valley regions to the Pyrenees and from the Mediterranean to the Danube.

The Visigoths
were loyal to Rome. They saved the West from the Huns and then drove the Vandals from Spain.

Jutes
Angles
Scotti
Frisians
Saxons
Britons
Burgundians
Alemanni
Lombards
Vandals
Franks
Ostrogoths ca.150–370
Vandals Alani 406–409
Visigoths 507–711
Visigoths 410
Vandals Alani 409–429
Vandals Alani 439–534

Ostrogoths and Lombards
alternately occupied Italy in the 6th century. The

Lombards, from Pannonia, were defeated by the Franks in the 8th century.

The Vandals
moved to Africa as they were driven from Spain. They, unlike other invaders, had a fleet.

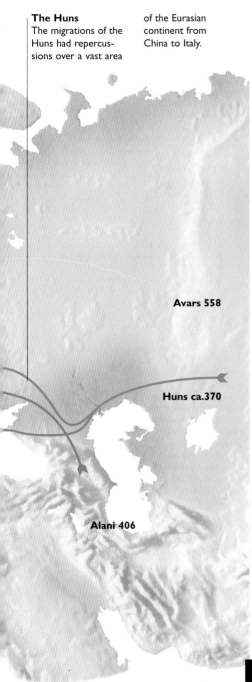

The Huns
The migrations of the Huns had repercussions over a vast area of the Eurasian continent from China to Italy.

Avars 558

Huns ca.370

Alani 406

erated rocks, trees, and other elements linked to a forest habitat. They made little use of iron and then only for producing weapons; war was in fact a permanent state of affairs among the Germanic tribes. Armed forays and raids into surrounding territories were frequent, and war and violence are recurring themes in their myths. The political structure of the Germans was based on the clan, a sort of extended family that constituted the basic social and economic unit in their society. From the Romans, the Germanic tribes had learned more advanced agricultural techniques. Those tribes that had penetrated into imperial territory actively sought assimilation into Roman society; in fact, Rome's institutionalized military system offered opportunities for accumulating honors and wealth that no barbarian society could match. During Rome's imperial age, the clash between the Germanic tribes with another group of nomads on the plains of Ukraine had radically transformed other peoples—Ostrogoths, Burgundians, Vandals, Gepis, and in part the Lombards—who came to be known as the Eastern Germans. They soon learned from the nomads the value of the horse in combat.

The Huns

For some time, the military superiority of the central Asian nomads had depended on their use of horses, their ability with the bow, their discipline, and the tactic of feigned retreat and ambush. In the fourth century,

The material culture of the Romano–Germanic kingdoms forms a bridge between ancient Roman culture and the younger and perhaps less refined and more primitive Germanic culture.

The cross
is the most important Christian symbol. From the Treasury of Guarrazar (Toledo), a Gothic votive cross in gold and precious stones.

The eagle
The Nordic peoples attributed a sacred character to nature and magical value to precious stones. Standards and weapons were gem-studded to intimidate the enemy and assist victory. Left, a gold buckle with almandines (6th–7th century). Germanisches Nationalmuseum, Nuremberg.

 the Huns moved through Asia into Europe and northern India. In Europe, some tribes clashed with the Eastern Germans, provoking a chain-reaction among the people they met. The Huns were a Turkish and Mongolian people of the central Asian steppes. Their organization, the horde, was a collection of migrating tribes answering to a single chief: Attila. He lived during the early fifth century, and is famous as the most ferocious of leaders. A warrior aristocracy formed the decision-making group. The horde, with its tendency to always be on the move, did not adapt well to establishing permanent settlements in the lands it occupied. The German migrations following the invasions of the central Asian nomads are conventionally taken as the point of passage, in

Merovingian art
Fifth-century glass
bottles from the
Merovingian times
(Musée des Antichités
nationales de
St.-Germain-en-
Laye).

Fusion of styles
The Visigothic church
of San Juan Bautista of
Baños de Cerrato
in Spain (7th–8th
century) is a fusion
of a Mediterranean
plan with Germanic
decorative elements.
This is evidence of
how styles and ideas
of the different peoples
intermingled.

Western cultural history, from the late ancient period to medieval times. Ethnic and cultural assimilation during this period was enormous. In the old Roman provinces of central and eastern Europe, along the Danube and as far as the Aegean Sea, barbarian cultures prevailed, while in Italy, Spain, Gaul, and in the West in general, the opposite happened: the barbarians became Romanized.

The Roman–Barbarian Kingdoms
The penetration of the Germanic peoples into the territories within the borders of the Western Roman Empire gave rise to a number of different kingdoms: the Vandals in Africa; the Visigoths in Spain; the Franks in Gaul; the Angles, the Jutes, and the Saxons in Britain; and the Ostrogoths in Italy formed the longest-lasting settlements. But, as we have said, it was

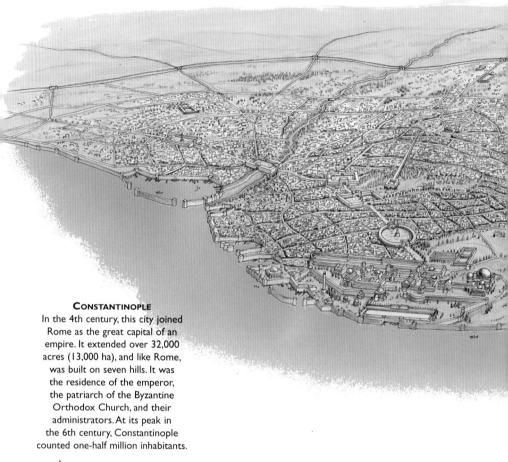

CONSTANTINOPLE
In the 4th century, this city joined Rome as the great capital of an empire. It extended over 32,000 acres (13,000 ha), and like Rome, was built on seven hills. It was the residence of the emperor, the patriarch of the Byzantine Orthodox Church, and their administrators. At its peak in the 6th century, Constantinople counted one-half million inhabitants.

more a migration (punctuated with episodes of violence and plunder by the barbarians, who were fascinated by the empire's cities of stone and brick and refined style of life) than a true military conquest. It was, all things considered, more a fusion than the domination of some peoples over others. The Germans became Christians. Their objective was not to overthrow Roman society or destroy its foundations, but rather, as long as they suc-

ceeded in keeping that society intact, to place their own warrior elite in leadership positions in the Roman administrative structure. The Vandal kingdom was the only one in which there was no cooperation between the Germanic invaders and the local population. The Vandals, Christians of the Arian Church, persecuted the followers of the Catholic faith. In all the Roman–Barbarian kingdoms, the economic and institutional foundations on which urban society rested were

Hagia Sophia
The most splendid of
the Eastern churches
was built between 532
and 537 on a square
plan by more than
10,000 workers.

slowly destroyed. There also came about a shift in society from the cities to rural areas. Slavery was replaced by serfdom typical of manorialism: the peasants, bound to the land, were subject to lords who were able to offer them military protection.

The Byzantine Empire

By the fourth century A.D., the Eastern Roman Empire was politically divided from the West. For this reason it had a different destiny. Its economic power, derived from its highly advantageous geographical position: Constantinople was the natural crossroads of trade routes linking East and West. It was there that major craft activities developed, producing mostly luxury products such as jewelry and textiles. The fabrics of Baghdad, Chinese silks, and the gems of India all found their way to Constantinople. The Eastern emperors succeeded in coming to terms with the Huns and the Germanic invaders by offering them tribute, and redirected their fury for conquest toward the West. The Byzantine Empire reclaimed it, created cultural and linguistic unity on the basis of Greek culture. It organized its own colossal state structure and elaborated its own policies. The most outstanding figure of the first centuries of the empire was without doubt Justinian I (r. 527–565), who attempted to restore the splendors of ancient Roman rule. He enacted a far-reaching reorganization of the Roman legal system, codified in his *Corpus Juris Civilis,* an immortal work that influenced law through many centuries to come. He also attempted

MILITARY MIGHT
The explosive strength of the Sasanid Empire lay with its highly organized and efficient army.

The third line
Elephants were arrayed behind the two formations of shock troops.

The second line
Immediately behind the heavy cavalry was a light cavalry of archers, all members of the minor nobility.

to reconquer the West by military force. All his efforts to oppose the Roman–Germanic kingdoms, however, eventually came to no avail.

The Sasanid Empire

All through its history, the Roman Empire had been threatened from the East by the kingdom of Parthia, the heir of the great Persian Empire, destroyed by Alexander the Great in the fourth century B.C. Its lands extended from the Persian plateau to Mesopotamia and to Syria. In A.D. 227, the Arsacid dynasty, which ruled in Parthia, was supplanted by the Sasanid dynasty of pure Persian descent. The policies of the Sasanids represented a turning point. The new

In the front line were the heavy armored cavalry provided by Persian nobles.

Bas-relief sculpture Above, the triumph of the Persian emperor Shapur over the Roman emperors Gordian III (trodden on by the horse), Philip the Arabian (kneeling), and Valerian (disarmed and led by the hand by Shapur). The symbolic value of the sculpture is evident.

THE GREAT ASIAN CIVILIZATIONS

While Europe was living in its Dark Ages, Turkish and Mongolian nomads threatened the peoples on its borders. Contemporary with the state of crisis and instability in the West, China, Japan, and India were enjoying a period of cultural splendor.

India

The Gupta dynasty consolidated a single empire that lasted from 320 to 550, and was followed by other Hindu regimes. Later Indian history was marked by disunity and Hindu resistance to Muslim expansion. Below, a Hindu temple.

TRANSFER

was the first method used for reproducing written characters. It spread through China starting in the 8th century.

1. The characters were engraved on a stone slab.

2. A sheet of dampened paper was applied to the engraved stone.

Paper

In China, the invention of paper and of ink (a mixture of pine carbon and plant-based glue) date to the 2nd century.

king reinstated the culture, the administrative structures, the political programs, and the religion of the ancient Persian Empire, sweeping away all the innovations introduced after the conquest of Alexander the Great. In particular, the Sasanid king demanded absolute respect for the doctrine of Zarathustra, the ancient prophet and father of the religion of the Medes and the Persians. He also instituted an aggressive policy toward the Romans. In the mid-third century, King Shapur I defeated, imprisoned, and executed the Roman emperor, Valerian. In the fifth century, the king of Persia was considered one of the most important leaders in the world, together with the emperor of the Eastern Roman Empire and the emperor of China.

China

Even the great Chinese Empire, at the Eastern edge of the world then known to the Europeans, felt the con- sequences of the movements of the central Asian nomads. Beginning in the third century B.C., they erected a great defensive wall more than 2,480 miles (4,000 km) in length. Between 202 B.C. and A.D. 220 the then-reigning Han dynasty had given government the imperial form that was destined to endure until the early twentieth century. Following the overthrow of

4. The dried paper was brushed with a blotter soaked in ink.

3. A cloth-covered hammer was used to press the paper against the stone.

Japan
The first permanent capital at Nara was established about 710, with great Buddhist temples including Todjai, dominated by the golden statue of Buddha. Buddhism was introduced from China in about 600.

the last Han emperor, China was divided into three parts; during a period when the Buddhist religion spread to all parts of China. In 618, the Tang dynasty came to power and by the ninth century had restored the empire to greatness. Chinese conquests in Korea and northern Vietnam created a Chinese cultural world over much of eastern Asia that survived the dynasty. In this period of its history, China was unusually open to trade with foreigners. Chinese porcelain was much appreciated throughout the Middle East, and refined Chinese silks were in great demand on the Constantinople market as well as in Baghdad and Córdobain Spain. The art of papermaking spread throughout the Islamic world, thanks to techniques learned from captured Chinese prisoners. Qangau, the capital of Tang China, was the largest city in Asia, even larger than Baghdad, the capital of the Abbasid Islamic Empire, which in that period reached the apex of its splendor.

Islam

The birth of Islam was the most important event in world history in the millennium between the fall of the Western Roman Empire and the sixteenth-century era of discovery. Islam, founded by the prophet Muhammad in the seventh century, provided the nomadic Bedouin tribes in the Arabian peninsula with a powerful element of cultural, linguistic, political, and economic unification. In less than a centu-

JERUSALEM
is the third holy city of the Islamic religion after Mecca, on the Arabian peninsula, where Muhammad was born in 570, and Medina, the city where he later lived. In Jerusalem, on the site of the Dome of the Rock, Muhammad is said to have ascended to heaven.

The Dome of the Rock
was built in 691 on the esplanade of the Temple of Solomon, destroyed by the Romans in A.D. 70.

The Qur'an
The sacred book of Islam, the Qur'an is a collection that Muslims believe to be the words of God transmitted orally by Muhammad. Certain disciples of the prophet gathered his sayings into 114 chapters, called suras.

The Five Pillars
Muslims must respect five basic tenets of faith:
1) Professing faith in no god but Allah.
2) Praying five times a day.
3) Fasting from dawn to dusk during the month of Ramadan.
4) Giving alms to the poor.
5) Making a pilgrimage to Mecca once in one's lifetime, if it is possible.

BAGHDAD
The splendid capital of the Abbasid Empire and today capital of Iraq was founded in 761 by Caliph al-Mansur (754–775).

The city
Many Muslim cities grew up around the main mosque and the different markets (suqs). The narrow alleys overflowed with shops and small craft establishments.

To market
In the Muslim markets, goods were sold in the open air. There were luxury items (silks, precious stones, pearls, perfumes, spices, dyes, ivory, gold, and slaves) and foodstuffs. Such fabrics as damask (typical of Damascus, woven of silk and cotton threads) and the cottons, silks, and wools of Mossul were much sought after.

ry, the influence of Islam had extended to a territory that went from Spain to the borders of the Chinese Empire and from the Caucasus Mountains to the Sahara Desert. It put heavy pressure on the Byzantine Empire and destroyed the Persian Sasanid Empire. Constantinople suffered two sieges, in 673 and 717. Islam did not proselytize among Jews and Christians, because Muhammad respected Judaism and Christianity and considered Abraham and Jesus his predecessors. Jews and Christians alike were free to practice their religions as long as they paid a special tax and built no new synagogues or churches.

Following Muhammad, political and religious power was administered by his successors, the Umayyad caliphs (661–750), who made their capital in Damascus in Syria. Their leaders were

The 1001 Arabian Nights
One of the caliphs of the Abbasid dynasty, Harun ar-Rashid (786–809), is the hero of many of the stories in this, the world-famous Arabic book. To this collection, compiled in definitive form in the 14th century, the Abbasid civilization contributed a wealth of stories centering on Baghdad. Left, a 13th-century Abbasid court scene.

responsible for the major territorial conquests. Even though the Umayyads controlled a vast area, the Muslim world was divided by political and religious struggles and independence movements. In 750, one of these exploded in an armed revolt guided by the family of the Abbasids, with Persian support, who took over the caliphate and held it until 1258. Islamic unity was shattered. The Umayyads fled to Spain, where they established an independent caliphate with Córdoba as its capital; the Fatimids founded kingdoms in North Africa, with Cairo (Egypt) as their capital; the Abbasids put their capital in Baghdad.

Due to the rapid expansion of Islam and the encounter of the Arab world with the Byzantine and Sasanid empires, in the beginning the administrative and political models and even the languages used in public documents were Greek, Coptic, and Persian. As Arab influence strengthened, however, the Arabic language began to dominate. The first gold and silver Muslim coins replaced the Byzantine coins still in circulation about A.D. 700. The use of a common idiom and centralized administration was from then on a distinct characteristic of the political constructions of the Muslim world. Magnificent cities were founded and a splendid culture flourished. Contacts with the Greek world favored the circulation of Arabic translations of Aristotle, Hippocrates, Galen, Euclid, and Ptolemy. The Arabs made decisive contributions to the fields of astronomy and mathematics, and their science and technology were destined to have considerable influence on the cultural advancement of Europe some centuries later. The numbers we use today, for example, are called "Arabic," and the number zero, fundamental for mathematical calculation, is of Indian derivation, but came to the West from the Arabs of Spain.

The Christian West

Between the fifth and tenth centuries, thanks to a blending of Germanic military traditions and Roman civilization, Western Europe acquired an original political and cultural conformation. The Christian religion was a preeminent factor in it. At its inception, Christianity was an urban phenomenon, while pagan cults continued to be rooted in the rural areas. Then, following the breakdown of

Monte Cassino rises on the summit of a mountain between Rome and Naples. The abbey was founded on the site of a pagan temple dedicated to Apollo. It was here in 529 where Saint Benedict built a dwelling place for his monks and an oratory.

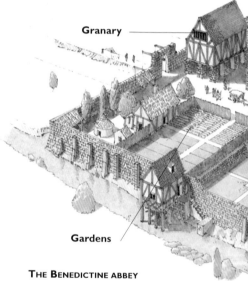

Granary

Gardens

THE BENEDICTINE ABBEY
The abbey, inspired by the rule of the life of Saint Benedict, was a complex and self-sufficient community.

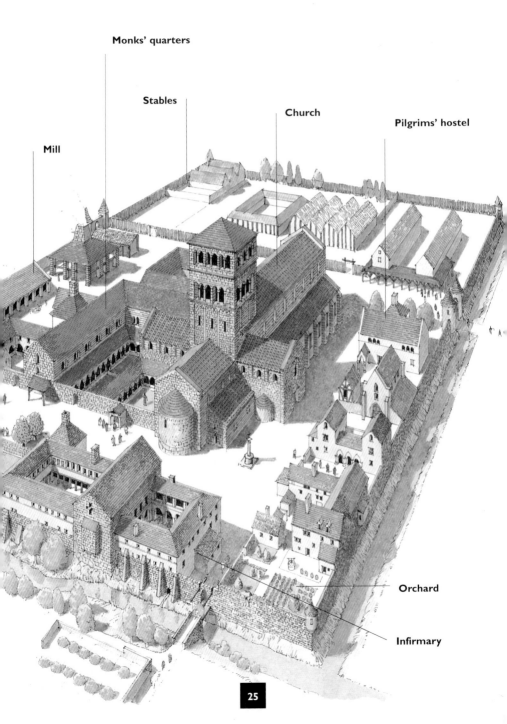

Monks' quarters

Stables

Church

Pilgrims' hostel

Mill

Orchard

Infirmary

25

the political structure of the Roman Empire, Christianity spread to many regions formerly under Roman dominion. The Church, which by that time was governed by city bishops, was an organization modeled on Roman administrative districts. The bishops stepped in to fill the power and administrative vacuums that were created as political leaders died or fled. Bishops' authority extended to the city in which they resided and its territories, that is, the diocese. During the entire European Middle Ages, bishops and cities were seldom thought of separately, and the Church made use of the ancient administrative structures of the empire to create its own. The great cities of the East—Jerusalem, Antioch, Alexandria, and Constantinople— were important episcopal centers, but the Bishop of Rome, the successor of Saint Peter and Saint Paul, held a primacy in the West. The monasticism of Saint Benedict of Nursia (480–549) was of extreme importance for the spread of Christianity, preservation of the cultural heritage of classical antiquity, and transmission of knowledge. Monasticism arose in its hermitic form (isolated individuals living solitary lives of prayer) in the Egyptian desert, but developed in a cenobitic form (religious groups living in common). In the monasteries inspired by the Rule of Saint Benedict (*ora et labora* = prayer and work), patient copyists saved works and manuscripts of the classical world from destruction. Other monks

THE BATTLE OF POITIERS
On October 12, 733, near Tours in southwestern France, an army of about 6,000 Franks under Charles Martel defeated a like number of Arabs led by Abd-ar-Rahaman. Many historians feel that this episode was decisive in halting Arab expansion into the West.

Abd-ar-Rahaman
was the governor of Córdoba, Spain, where the Muslims had ruled since 711. He was defeated in France, and this contributed to convincing the Muslim rulers of the Umayyad dynasty to halt their expansion at the Pyrenees.

The Frankish cavalry
Charles Martel organized squadrons of horsemen, more agile than foot-soldiers. He may have guessed the importance of the stirrup (already in use by Byzantines and Muslims) in improving the rider's seat and thus allowing him to apply more force to his lance thrust.

Charles Martel
(689–741)
From mayor of the palace of the Frankish kingdom of Austrasia in the Merovingian realm consolidated by Clovis I in the late 5th century, Charles Martel rose to become sole governor. The official passage from the Merovingian dynasty to the Carolingian came about only in 750 under one of Charles Martel's sons, Pepin III the Short.

The Frankish infantry was protected by large, heavy teardrop shields.

opened new ground and transformed small garden plots into large farms, contributing to later repopulation and new forms of organized community life.

In some areas, the Christian religion spread quietly, as in the British Isles, where many missionaries worked; in other cases, with violence, as in Saxony under the weapons of the Franks, the most powerful of the Germanic kingdoms of that time.

The "Carolingian Renaissance"

In the year 800, Charles I, king of the Franks, received the crown of the Roman Empire from the hands of Pope Leo III. The idea of a great universal empire had not been forgotten with the fall of the Western part of the Roman Empire. The emperor of the East obviously considered himself the legitimate heir to the sovereign dignity of times past, but he reigned over only the Greek portion of the territory. Charles's empire, while Catholic, was Frankish, with its axis in the Rhine Valley and Charles himself was a "barbarian." The notion of a Roman Empire, from the Byzantine point of view, was destined to endure: it sanctioned the unification of, under the Franks, civil and religious authority, an alliance that soon produced serious conflicts. It failed to provide boundaries between the competencies of an emperor who was also a religious leader and a pope who headed his own state and was therefore a political as well as spiritual leader.

From his court in the Roman spa of Acquisgranum (Aachen, which probably did not exceed 2,000 inhabitants

The throne
was placed in a
high position under-
neath an immense
mosaic of Christ.
To everyone's eyes,
Charlemagne was
the mediator
between God and
the community
of the faithful.

The *Missi Dominici*
In order to govern
such a vast empire,
Charlemagne
divided it into
regions entrusted
to counts. The
counts were in
turn inspected by
the missi, trusted
and powerful men
with full investigatory
powers.

THE MOORS
In the 9th century, Muslim populations of North Africa conducted raids along the European coasts and then into the interior. Rome fell victim to a Muslim raid in 846.

In France,
in about 890, a group of Muslims from Spain landed in a small village of the Côte d'Azur called Fraxinetum ("ash-grove"). Given the strategic position of the village, the pirates made it their headquarters and from here set out on a series of raids that terrorized the entire coast. Above, the castle of Miramas-les-Vieux.

at the time), Charlemagne restored to written documents the functions they had under the Roman Empire, so that orders arrived accurately to officials. A literate bureaucracy was thus called for. Secondly, as spiritual leader, Charlemagne wanted to spread religious instruction and therefore promoted the education of the clergy. In short, Charlemagne transformed the court from a warrior camp into an active center of culture and began that substantial work of renewal that is known as the Carolingian Renaissance.

The last invasions of Europe
The relatively stable government of the Carolingian dynasty in central Europe guaranteed a certain sense of security to the religious and mercantile communities. In this climate, the eighth-century abbeys and markets were left undefended and the ancient

The raids
The Muslims sacked and plundered the territories they entered and formed permanent settlements only rarely. Above all, they carried off precious metals, valuable objects, and men and women whom they sold as slaves in the Arab world.

Roman fortifications were in utter neglect and ruin. But the concentrations of wealth in these places attracted raiders from far away, men who brushed aside the authority of Christian kings and laughed at the religious sanctions that were intended to protect the sacred Christian sites. In the ninth and tenth centuries, Europe was attacked by three groups of invaders: Arab and Berber Muslims, the Hungarians, and the Vikings.

The Muslims
The raids of the Muslims from North Africa were more than anything else attempts at expansion. Following the occupation of Sicily—ending in 827—Muslim pirates established bases along the Italian coast and then in southern Gaul, from where they were able to threaten vast areas of Europe. Corsica and Sardinia were attacked many times and monasteries and cities in Italy (including Rome) and in Gaul were

THE VIKINGS IN PARIS
Near the end of the 9th
century, the empire created by
Charlemagne was in difficulty.
Between 885 and 886, Paris was
raided by Danish Vikings.

The bridges
Paris was linked to dry
land by two bridges,
one in stone and one
in wood. The collapse
of the wooden bridge
made it easy for the
Vikings to sail up the
Seine to raid the sur-
rounding countryside.

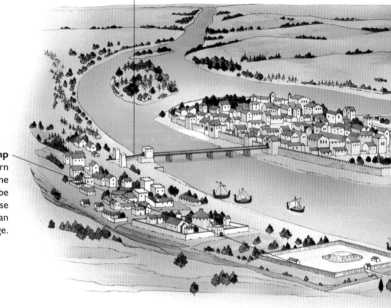

The Viking camp
on the northwestern
bank of the Seine
proved to be
a better base
for raids than
for a true siege.

sacked. Pilgrims and mer-
chants were robbed or made
prisoners. Byzantine troops
were called in to drive the pirates from
their bases in Italy.

The Vikings

Another invasion had quite a different impact on Europe. This time it
was the Vikings (Northmen), peoples
from isolated Denmark, Norway, and
Sweden who attacked Western
Europe. All three were Germanic peoples who in the early Christian era
sailed the seas on oar-driven ships
and established profitable trade relations with the Roman world. They
appeared on the continent between
650 and 800. They made use of special
types of ships that allowed them to
sail both along the coastline and
across the oceans—and when neces-
sary, to sail upriver into the interior.
The migrations of the Scandinavians
often followed the great international
trade routes. Some headed toward the
Ukrainian steppes, where they played
an important part in the birth of the

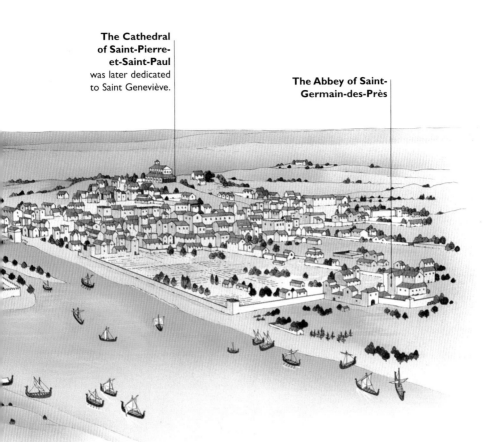

The Cathedral of Saint-Pierre-et-Saint-Paul was later dedicated to Saint Geneviève.

The Abbey of Saint-Germain-des-Près

first Russian state. There they came into contact with the Byzantine and Muslim worlds; other Northmen set out east toward Iceland and reached the American continent; still others descended the Atlantic coast of Europe to the Mediterranean. In the years 859–860, bands of Vikings attacked London, York, Rouen, Nantes, and then Seville, Cadiz, Barcelona, the Balearic Islands, the towns of southern Provence, and Luni and Pisa in Italy. They began as pagan destroyers bent on plundering, but soon created political institutions and exacted tribute from subject peoples. They also became Christians. In the ninth century, one group, the Normans, settled in northern France in the region that takes its name from them: Normandy. From here, the Norman duke William I the Conqueror set out in the eleventh century for England.

In the meantime, the Viking influence had destabilized the Carolingian Empire and had considerable consequences on the social and military reorganization of the West: building

Trade

In the extensive markets created in Ukraine and Russia by the Scandinavians, Nordic products such as furs and narwhale tusks were traded for wax and amber and the bronzes and silks of China, spices and ceramics, jewels, and weapons of Islamic manufacture.

Viking ships

The Vikings exploited navigable rivers to penetrate the interior of the continent. If required, they could lower the mast, pull in the oars, raise the rudder with a hawser, and slide the boat overland on a bed of tree trunks to the next river.

In the 9th–10th century, the Vikings subdued the eastern Slavic populations and occupied their major centers (Novgorod and Kiev), forming a single great principality called Rus, with its capital at Kiev.

castles and initiating a new social and economic system, known as feudalism.

The Hungarians

The third great invasion of Europe in the tenth century was by the Hungarians, a people speaking a language of Turkic origin and like the Huns of five centuries earlier, once were central-Asian nomads. They settled in the steppes of Pannonia, in the region later to be known as Hungary. Like those of the Huns, the Hungarians' raids were conducted for booty rather than to conquer new territories. In 937, they reached the outskirts of Paris and sacked Burgundy and the Rhone Valley. Cities usually resisted the Hungarian horsemen, who used stirrups but were too lightly armed to effectively attack and lay siege to a city. The Hungarians therefore preferred devastating the countryside and sacking the monasteries. The Hungarian movement was slowed in part by the Saxon kings who then ruled the Holy Roman Empire, but more by their own progressive loss of momentum, until the Hungarians became permanently based stock-raisers. Their conversion to Christianity was the final step in their integration among the newly forming Western European nations. In the year 1000, King Stephan received a crown for Hungary from Pope Sylvester II.

The Slavs

In the history of the population of Europe during the first millennium A.D., an important chapter is reserved for the Slavic peoples who were little known to

Kiev became the capital of a vast principality founded by Oleg, a 9th-century Swedish Viking. Before long it was one of Europe's most important centers of trade, culture, and art.

the Romans and successive civilizations. We presume they originated in an isolated area, probably between the Vistula River in Poland and the Dnieper River in Ukraine. And here they stayed, until in the sixth century, Asian peoples pushed the western Slavs (Poles, Czechs, Slovaks) into contact with the Germanic world. The eastern Slavs, the Russians, Ukrainians, and Byelorussians, and the southern Slavs, Serbs, Croats, and Slovenes, and the Bulgars, a people of Turkic origin later consolidated with the Slavs, turned toward Byzantium. For the Slavs, as for the Germans, long before them, integration into European society came about through the conversion of their leaders to Christianity. The profession of a single religion also represented a strong element of unification, cohesion, and identity among the different Slavic populations.

In the late ninth century, around the trade center of Kiev, a nucleus formed that was to become Ukraine. A century later Kiev embraced Byzantine Christianity thanks to the conversion of Prince Vladimir, who had stipulated an alliance with Constantinople. The early Polish state, instead, espoused the teachings of missionaries from Rome, as did the duchy of Bohemia in the ninth and tenth centuries. Czechs, Slovenes, and Croats turned to the Church of Rome; Serbs and Bulgarians to the Church of Constantinople.

The Ottonian Dynasty
Though it was the Slavs who pressured the Byzantine Empire, and in whose

The pagan god
Soldiers of the prince threw the statue of the pagan deity Perun into the Dnieper, the river of Kiev, in a symbolic gesture rejecting the false gods.

THE BAPTISM OF PRINCE VLADIMIR
In order to make his state a modern country, the pagan prince Vladimir of Kiev (956–1015) sought an alliance with the Byzantine Empire. He converted to Christianity and forced his people to do the same.

AN IMPERIAL WEDDING
In 972, the marriage of Otto II of Germany and the Byzantine princess Theophano was celebrated in Saint Peter's Basilica in Rome. It was the intention of the Saxon dynasty that the marriage seal the rapprochement of the Byzantine and the Holy Roman Empires.

Balkan territories some of their tribes had settled, it was the Vikings, the Hungarians, and the Muslims who created crisis in the empire created by Charlemagne. It had already been weakened by the Frankish custom of dividing up kingdoms among various sons following the death of their father.

The empire, in the German, French, and Italian territories, was thus made up of a myriad of small principalities. It was literally pulverized, with the principalities often at war with each other. In 936, a half-century after the end of the Carolingian Empire, Otto I became king of Germany and in 955 acquired great prestige among Christians by defeating the Hungarians in a pitched battle at Lechfeld, in southern Germany. He consolidated his power to the detriment of the great feudal vassals, who with the dissolution of the Carolingian Empire had taken to gov-

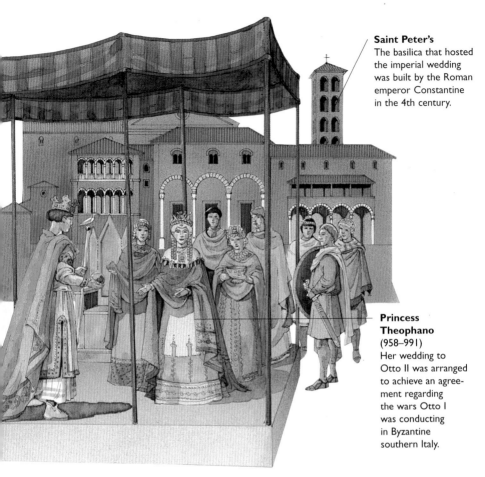

erning their territories as though they were so many small independent states. In 962, Otto I of Saxony was crowned Holy Roman Emperor; 11 days later, he issued the Privilegium Ottonianum, by which no pope could be consecrated without the prior approval of the Holy Roman Emperor.

Otto's system of government employed the bishops as imperial officers. This confusion between civil and religious powers was destined to create intense contrasts between the pope and the emperor, the two highest authorities in the Western political world during the Middle Ages. The Ottonian dynasty gave the empire a decidedly Germanic cast and the emperor himself, adding to the changes introduced by Charlemagne, became someone "anointed by the Lord." Society as a whole was Christian, and it was divided into three broadly defined classes.

FARMERS, KNIGHTS, AND MONKS

Beginning in the tenth century, economic power and a social structure known as "feudalism" spread throughout Europe. The three classes of the feudal order were those who possessed the land, those who farmed it, and those who prayed.

The European crisis

The invasions of the Vikings had left Western Europe fractured politically, depopulated, and impoverished. The forests that had again encroached upon the cultivated lands were the people's major resource. The small plots of land they succeeded in clearing (mostly with simple axes) and cultivating produced modest agricultural yields. Some innovations had been introduced: the water mill, known to the Romans, had made it possible to put water energy to better use, the horse collar permitted better exploitation of animal energy, a new type of plow (introduced in the seventh or eightth century) that cut deeper and turned over soil had improved har-

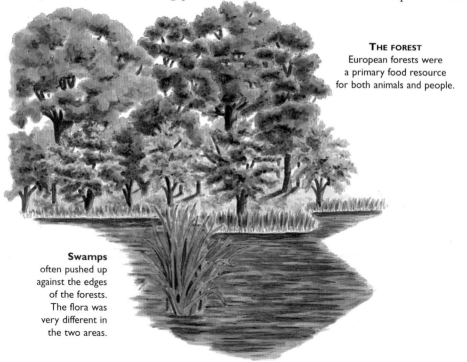

THE FOREST
European forests were a primary food resource for both animals and people.

Swamps often pushed up against the edges of the forests. The flora was very different in the two areas.

vests. A new type of annual rotation of the cultivated fields ensured fodder for the animals needed for farmwork. Agricultural productivity nevertheless remained low. By and large, the land was farmed for simple sustenance and little or nothing remained for market.

The population of Europe was often decimated by famines and epidemics and in the tenth century was probably at its lowest level since the fall of the Western part of the Roman Empire. In the year 1000, it numbered an estimated 30 million. In the depopulated cities,

The European hornbeam
This tree, growing to 80 feet (25 m), was used for firewood.

The oak produces acorns, and in the medieval forests was one of the few trees that were replanted.

Wild boars base their diet on acorns, and in the oak forests are completely self-sufficient.

The underwood, abounding in mushrooms and many wild fruits, was another source of sustenance.

AGRICULTURAL INNOVATIONS
A series of improvements in the utilization of energy, cultivation techniques, and technology underlay the betterment of European agriculture that started about the year 1000.

The water mill
The energy supplied by running water was systematically exploited from the 6th century on.

trade was practically nonexistent, and crafts were at a low level.

The agricultural revolution

With the close of invasions in the eleventh century, the situation in Western Europe began to change. The most spectacular phenomenon was a population boom that went hand in hand with what was more an increase in agricultural production in absolute terms than of productivity. Underlying progress in the West was the "agricultural revolution," which consisted of the revival and wide-scale implementation of "forgotten" farming techniques and in a sizeable increase in the acreage under cultivation. The revolution took three basic forms: intense ground-breaking by the peasants of the old villages at the edges of the woods that surrounded their fields; migration of farm-workers toward the uninhabited highlands and mountains, where they began carving scattered holdings and small fields out of the woods and forests; and planned development by the feudal lords or the monks, who founded hamlets and villages at the foot of castles or alongside monasteries. The resources of the dominant social classes were fundamental to this revolution, which they largely financed. For example, large reclamation projects were undertaken, which could never have succeeded without the investment of the great landowners.

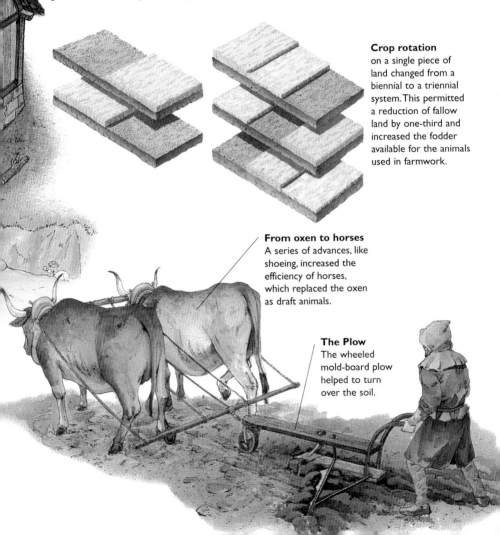

Crop rotation
on a single piece of land changed from a biennial to a triennial system. This permitted a reduction of fallow land by one-third and increased the fodder available for the animals used in farmwork.

From oxen to horses
A series of advances, like shoeing, increased the efficiency of horses, which replaced the oxen as draft animals.

The Plow
The wheeled mold-board plow helped to turn over the soil.

Firing
was a method often used for deforestation. Although it destroyed the wood, the land was enriched with no need for additional fertilizer for several years.

DEFORESTATION
Cleared lands were used for pasture or immediately planted with grain.

Wood
The felled trees were used for farm buildings and rural dwellings; the shrubby portions and the less valuable wood as fuel.

Felling
Since burning, although it fertilized the soil, destroyed the wood, from the 12th century onward the most common method of deforestation was felling with axes, saws, and billhooks.

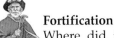

Fortification

Where did the great lords live? But first, a premise. The Carolingian dynasty, in order to blunt the invasions of the Muslims, the Vikings, and the Hungarians and to govern an empire that in the ninth century embraced a good part of Europe, drew on a cultural heritage of the Frankish world. Personal ties united a king and his followers. In exchange for an oath of loyalty, the Carolingian kings had granted benefices (that is, lands) to trusted men in order that the latter would have the resources for arming themselves. This bond, based on an oath of fealty and the benefice, was called vassalage and subordinated the vassal to his lord. Originally a means of conscription, it became a method of governing. The loyal vassal who administered a territory for the king obtained other benefices, for example the enjoyment of the taxes collected in the territory, or particular immunities and exemptions. Over time the vassals of the king, counts, and marquises became lords, who in turn ruled over lesser vassals from whom they too received an oath and to whom they granted a benefice. Around the year 1000, we find one of these smaller vassals living in a castle surrounded by a fortified wall. He needs a workforce, because he has to clear and till the land he has been granted. He can provide the tools, which are now more efficient. Thus peasants, previously scattered throughout the countryside, come to him in search of both work and protection. The lord of the castle grants use of the land to the peasants, and in exchange demands a good part of their harvests; he also demands that the tenant-farmer, besides working the land he has received in benefice, also work the land in which he has retained the rights of direct possession and exploitation. At this stage, the castle was basically a closed economy with only sporadic outside contacts. With still very little money in circulation, trade was mainly in goods (lands and harvests) and services (work shifts in the lords' fields).

A major change came about when the benefice granted the lord of the castle (that is, the vassal who had first received the land) into a hereditary fief. He no longer simply possessed the land—it became his property. The feud or fief was an absolute dominion, and the lord had the faculty to judge and to mete out punishment, exercising the political power that the authority of the state (the king or the emperor) could

THE CASTLE
The structure of the castle changed from the 9th to the 14th centuries. From a simple stronghold housing the garrison, it became the private residence of the lord as well as his political and administrative center. The Tyrol Castle is an example of this evolution.

In the 9th century
the castle was a simple enclosure with crenellated walls built atop a hill. The vassal-holders lived outside of it, for it was then only a garrison.

In the 13th century, new higher and stronger defensive walls and a residential wing for the vassal and his family were added. The struggle against the nobility had begun.

In the 14th century, the architecture of the castle became more complex, when spaces used by the vassal as headquarters for his activities were added.

THE SEAT OF POWER
During the last phase of its
evolution, the castle became
the seat of the lord's
political and social
activities. He received
ambassadors, administered
justice, and held sumptuous
receptions.

The chapel,
built in the residential
wing, was an
important element
of the castle. At the
time, the clergy were
the only educated
class and therefore
performed adminis-
trative functions.

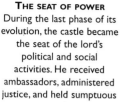

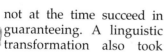

not at the time succeed in guaranteeing. A linguistic transformation also took place: the Medieval Latin term of Germanic origin *feodum*, which in the late ninth century was synonymous with simple benefice, came to signify a hereditary benefice. The castle, an essential element in the feudal organization of the tenth century, became the center of a small independent territorial state with full powers: economic, juridical, and political.

The three orders of society

The men of the feudal world were well aware of the fact that their society was divided into three classes. There were those who possessed land and the means to maintain a horse

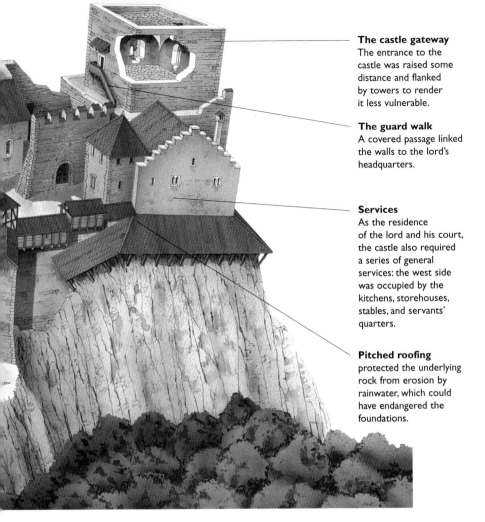

The castle gateway
The entrance to the castle was raised some distance and flanked by towers to render it less vulnerable.

The guard walk
A covered passage linked the walls to the lord's headquarters.

Services
As the residence of the lord and his court, the castle also required a series of general services: the west side was occupied by the kitchens, storehouses, stables, and servants' quarters.

Pitched roofing
protected the underlying rock from erosion by rainwater, which could have endangered the foundations.

and battle equipment: the knights. Then there were the peasants or farmers, freedmen or serfs, who worked the land: the farm workers. And finally, there were the church men and women.

The nobility and the knights
The nobles owed their privileged condition to the fact that they possessed the land they had received as a benefice from the king. Since the Carolingian era, they had used the land to become men-at-arms in the service of their ruler, and later his administrators. In the ninth century, when the foot soldiers lost their decisive edge in battle, these men-at-arms took to horseback and became professional cavalry warriors. By the tenth century, the warriors

had gained in prestige and lords and knights shared a common lifestyle; the knight was thus likened to the noble. Because of the hereditary nature of benefices, the feudal lords became a closed order: nobles were no longer made on merit or by appointment, they were born. In order to reinforce their power over a territory, to consolidate it, and to assure its transmission, the nobility adopted a power structure based on male lineage from a common ancestor; that is, the rightful heir was the firstborn son of the lord. The younger sons were elevated to the rank of knight in a formal ritual that included the awarding of the knightly equipment and the ceremonial dubbing. In the twelfth and thirteenth centuries, the dubbing ceremony came to be reserved exclusively for the sons of knights. Thus the nobility in

A BANQUET AT THE CASTLE
One of the favorite pastimes at the medieval court was the banquet. In splendid halls decorated and illuminated for the occasion, conversing to the accompaniment of music, the diners enjoyed dinner menus centering on game dishes.

The lord's new clothes
However small or lacking in amenities a castle might have been, the lord wore elegant clothes, especially on important occasions.

Entertainers
Musicians and jesters entertained the guests at banquets. The jesters were often permitted to express bitter truths in a humorous manner, a liberty the lord allowed no one else.

The Templars were the prototype of the "soldiers of Christ," military-religious order. The order of the Templars was founded about 1119 for defending the territories conquered by the crusaders in the Holy Land.

the late Middle Ages was a rigidly defined order both at its top (the lords of the castles) and in the lower ranks of plain knights, who were in the lords' service and sometimes had barely enough to live on. With time, the knighthood developed a precise code of conduct, almost an ideology, called chivalry. The fact that the knight was generally bound to a lord from whom he had received a benefice in exchange for loyalty discouraged the figure of the "knight errant," that transcended the social context of the times. The solitary knight without a fief became a major figure of the chivalric romances, the *chansons de geste* produced in France after the year 1000. Like the *Chanson de Roland,* they exalted the ideals of chivalry: generosity, liberality, and the valor of the knight, who in the absence of an established power was committed to quelling conflicts and to acting as protector of the weak and defenseless against tyrants. As society became more strongly Christianized, the knight assumed an almost sacred function. He was the soldier of Christ, who would battle the Muslims for control of the Holy Land.

The farmers

Even before the ninth-century era of extensive clearing, the European peasant was either a freeman who cultivated his own land for subsistence or a tenant in the service of a lord who had rented him land. The economic conditions of the two types of peasant farmers were different. There also existed a

THE JOUST
Tournaments and jousts were among the most intense moments of the life of the medieval aristocracy. During these contests, the nobles gave elegant proof of their strength and courage.

The squires
The great knights were accompanied by squires, servants who carried their weapons. The knights' personnel was housed in tents.

The knight, at the moment of his investiture, took on a series of duties that went from defending the Church at the cost of his own life to that of combating evil in all its forms.

clear distinction between the family's "plowmen" who possessed beasts of burden and the "hands" who were forced to till the soil with only a hoe. The tenants were obliged to deliver part of their harvest to the lord and to perform certain servile functions for him.

The condition of the peasants improved during the agricultural revolution, when much new land was opened for cultivation and agricultural production increased. Hereditary subdivisions and improved harvests had broken up the large land-holdings where the peasants had flocked to work the land. The corvées (the forced service the farmers were required to provide to the lord), had decreased, but the labor

The hoist
In order to mount his horse, the 14th-century warrior was forced to make use of a windlass-hoist operated by the knight's squires and attendants. The heavier armor of the late Middle Ages reduced the agility of the cavalry in battle.

dues of the tenants were commuted into cash rents as soon as coins began to circulate. Overall, the lords increased their demands, and forced them to comply because they had the authority to take away their farms. Besides handing down justice, the lord required his tenants to make use of his mills and ovens, and set a whole series of impositions that replaced those required by the king's officials during the Carolingian era.

The local lord's authority was naturally all the stronger, but it was also easier to resist, in a sense. The lord enforced what he felt were his rights, but if he wanted workers for his fields, he also had to make some concessions to those who cleared and farmed them. Franchises, for example, put down in written form the new rights that the farmers wanted to protect, like the right to sell the land that had been granted them (which proved to be a decisive step toward full ownership), or the right to grind their grain on their own, bypassing use of the mills of the lord and thus escaping strict control of production and new taxes.

The new villages

The peasants gravitated around the castle, called in by the vassal who needed laborers. Near the castle the peasant felt protected, and the vassal's role of guarantor of justice and order was a perfect substitute for a distant and disinterested imperial authority. Thus was born the village or hamlet: small collections of

THE HOME
For the medieval peasant, the home was a mere shelter, since the majority of his activities were carried on out-of-doors.

Domestic animals
Medieval men and women often shared their living space with their domestic animals, which were stabled near the entrance.

The roof
was a wooden frame
covered with thatch;
in the more highly
developed areas,
some roofs were
slate-covered.

Food
The medieval diet
featured a variety
of fish and cereals
(in the form of
bread and flatcakes);
meats such as
chicken and beef
were seldom to
be had.

houses in the immediate vicinity of the castle, or near a large land-holding, and often founded on the lord's own initiative. Each village was surrounded by an area of between 740 and 2470 acres (300 and 1000 ha). The products of the earth were in part destined for consumption by the farmers themselves; another part of the production was surplus in that it was delivered to the lord as tribute and later found its way into city markets. The names of a great many villages founded in this period indicate their recent constitution or their particular legal status. We thus have the Italian Villanova or the French Villeneuve, both meaning "new city," and the Italian Villafranca or German Freistadt, meaning "free city," which obviously had obtained the right to self-government by gift or purchase. The founding of new villages, often on a grid plan, proceeded hand in hand with the reconstruction and expansion of the old cities.

The churchmen

The third great order of the feudal world was that of the clergy, monks and nuns, those who pray. They fell into two groups, the clergy, who looked after the faithful on orders from the local bishop, and the monks. As in the other categories of society, deep-seated social differences also existed among the churchmen. The country priest was of humble origin; the member of the chapter of a cathedral drew wealth from his fiefs and came from a powerful noble family. It was similar in the monasteries, espe-

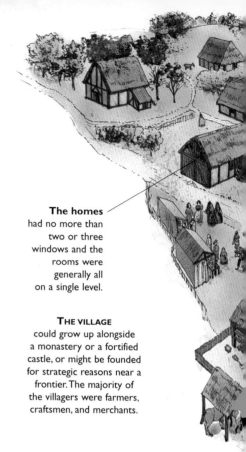

The homes had no more than two or three windows and the rooms were generally all on a single level.

THE VILLAGE could grow up alongside a monastery or a fortified castle, or might be founded for strategic reasons near a frontier. The majority of the villagers were farmers, craftsmen, and merchants.

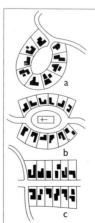

The plan of a medieval village
Although village plans varied according to area, the houses in newly founded settlements generally followed a regular plan centering on a church (a and b) or along a road or forest track (b and c). The common uncultivated lands and the forest extended around it.

The streets
were narrow to permit better defense of the built-up area and to save space.

The church
At the center of the village, the church towered over all the other buildings. It was generally the only stone building in the village.

cially in the twelfth century: there were the monks, who dedicated their time to prayer and generally came from families of knights, and lay brothers, who performed specific duties and were of peasant origin.

We have already seen how, beginning in the sixth century, the abbeys exerted a stabilizing influence in a period in which all the political institutions had collapsed. They also participated actively in the feudal system. For example, the Benedictine Abbey of Corbie in France—whose scriptorium issued some of the best-known manuscripts of the Carolingian era—kept 150 specialized servants whose only task was to carry food to the community of monks.

The superiors aimed at producing all they needed to live in the abbeys themselves and on adjacent land. Not only the regular clergy (that is, those following a rule set down by a founder), but also the secular clergy, who served a bishop, were active participants in the life of this world.

Through donations, the Church became one of the largest real-estate owners in the Western world. The donations were often from the nobles, who in this manner intended to make "private" churches of those they financed. They might, for instance, appoint one of their servants as clergyman, or personally collect rents attached to the church's property. This type of interference between the nobility and the ecclesiastical world, which mirrored the contrasts of jurisdiction between the pope and the emperor, was

THE ABBEY CHURCH OF CLUNY, founded in 910 in Burgundy (France), was enlarged between 955 and 991 and again in 1088. It was almost entirely destroyed between 1809 and 1823.

The *Scholae Cantorum,* medieval singing schools and associated choirs, supplied professional singers who performed a repertoire of monophonic liturgical music called plainsong or Gregorian chant.

The Cluniac order
The lifestyle of this monastic order was modeled on the Benedictine Rule. It intended to recover its fundamental values. About 1100, the Cluniac order had 1450 houses with 10,000 monks; 815 were in France, 109 in Germany, 52 in Italy, 43 in the British Isles, and 23 in Spain. Right, the Abbey of Cluny around the year 1000.

The *scriptorium* of an abbey was a room adjacent to the library where the patient work of copying texts was carried on.

WORK IN THE ABBEY
Reform of daily routine and the
organization of the monasteries
contributed, in the 10th–12th
century, to the spiritual renewal
of Benedictine monasticism. At
Cluny, many hours of the day
were dedicated to prayer and
intellectual labors, while manual
work as delegated to serfs.

Power and opulence
Cluny was the largest religious building in the West, and the abbot of Cluny was the second most important religious figure, after the pope. Cluny's storehouses were filled to overflowing.

The Cistercians
The Cistercian order stood out for its devotion to a life of poverty. The Cistercian buildings and the abbey furnishings were extremely plain. Above, the Cistercian Abbey of Sénanque in Provence (France), founded in the 12th century.

 destined to favor loss of freedom outside and discipline within the Church.

Cluniac and Cistercian monasticism

Churches and monastic communities were large landowners and therefore participated in the economic and political organization of the land. Naturally, the cultural and spiritual orientations of the nobles and churchmen were different. The Abbey of Cluny, founded in 910 in Burgundy by Duke William the Pious of Aquitaine, intended to put into practice the ancient Benedictine Rule. Above all it urged its monks to follow the contemplative life and detachment from worldly matters. From its founding, Cluny was "exempted" from the powers of the bishop of nearby Macon, and this freed the abbey of the influence of aristocratic families and protected it against economic decline. The abbey acquired lands and immunities through all of Europe. It had the right to set up a permanent organization of priories, all bound by a bond of solidarity to the parent house at Cluny. The monasteries, inspired by the Benedictine Rule of Cluny, answered directly to the pope, who was far away, and offered support when aid was required for launching the reform of the Church.

The Rule of Saint Benedict was interpreted differently by the monks of the Abbey of Citeaux, whose most famous abbot was Saint Bernard de Clairvaux (1090–1153). The Cistercians intended to fully recover that lifestyle of poverty and manual labor that at Cluny had been relegated to second place. They condemned the feudal dominion and the exploitation of the serfs typical of the great monastic and ecclesiastical properties. If the Cluniac monasteries were given well-tended fields or good land to be cleared by the serfs, the Cistercians were given swampy lands that the monks themselves reclaimed.

The pilgrimages

The Cluniac and the Cistercian monks were only the two most striking examples of a great spiritual reform movement that pervaded the Church in the eleventh century. Christian society began to feel the need for a church free from the interests of the great feudal domains, a church that was more attentive to the spiritual aspects of life—more evangelical, in a word. In this context, the figure of the pilgrim represented the freedom enjoyed by someone who is free to move without constrictions.

The devotional practice of pilgrimage has been practiced in many ages and in many different cultures. In the Christian world, it was connected with the idea of life as a journey toward eternity, along an itinerary of purification. Rome and Jerusalem have been destinations for pilgrims since the first centuries of the Christian era, but pilgrimage received an enormous stimulus in the early ninth century. The presumed discovery of the tomb of the Apostle James in Compostela, Spain elicited a flow of pilgrims from every part of Europe, rich and poor alike, who set out after having made their wills and having participated in a ritu-

The basilica built around the tomb of Saint James and consecrated in 899, was totally transformed during the Romanesque period.

SANTIAGO DE COMPOSTELA

After Rome, Compostela was the most important destination in Western Europe for medieval pilgrims. The legend says that the remains of Saint James the Apostle, decapitated in A.D. 44 in Jerusalem, were transferred to Galicia. The presumed tomb of the Apostle came to light in the early 11th century, and was recognized as such due to the blinding light that enveloped it (hence the name Compostela, from ad campus stellae).

The roads

Most of the medieval roads were built by the Romans, and the itineraries of the pilgrims also followed the Roman routes. Some new roads were nevertheless opened by merchants and pilgrims. Above, a stretch of the Via Cassia.

The pilgrims

The pilgrim wore a wide-brimmed hat for protection from the sun and carried a walking-stick and a shoulder-slung backpack. A shell affixed to the hat or the cloak identified the traveler as a pilgrim to Compostela.

63

Very few people could read
or write in the Middle Ages.
Transmission of the articles of
the faith was mostly entrusted
to images. The decorations of
the portals of the churches
had great impact on the
pilgrims' imagination.

**The Church of
Saint-Lazare**
The tympanum of the
portal was sculpted
by Master Gislebertus
in 112–135. Christ
the Judge is at the
center, between the
elect and the damned.

 al. The obligatory way sta-
tions of any pilgrimage are
churches, basilicas, and
chapels containing the real or presumed relics of a saint or martyr. In the
Middle Ages, the desire for a hands-on
type of spirituality was strong. The
cult of the relics induced multitudes to
visit the sanctuaries, which in turn
helped spread religious beliefs. It

above all increased contact between
different cultures, languages, lifestyles, and ideas. Europe had begun to
take on an identity of its own, and it
was a Christian identity.

The rebirth of sculpture
The eleventh and twelfth centuries saw
the coming to maturity of an art that
had every right to call itself "European":

The damned
The souls of the damned
are pulled down into Hell
by huge grasping hands.

The elect
The souls of just men
are raised to heaven
by angelic figures.

Sculptural subjects
The aim of the sculpted
images on Romanesque
church portals was to
attract the faithful
and, like a sermon,
communicate the
fundamental tenets
of Christian life.

the Romanesque style, known as the Norman style in England. The term "Romanesque" links the style with the Latin tradition, but the evocation of Rome is more a synonym for culture and an appeal to Church tradition than a backward glance. Romanesque art is, in fact, an essentially religious art. As Europe began on its way to a new sense of well-being, the centers of inter- est began to move away from the cas- tles and the great feudal land-holdings to the cities, and the cities responded. Europe began to fill with new churches and basilicas, but also restored monas- teries and village churches. Whether majestic or humble, built in the hearts of cities or in small villages, the Romanesque basilicas were true books made of stone. The majority of the peo-

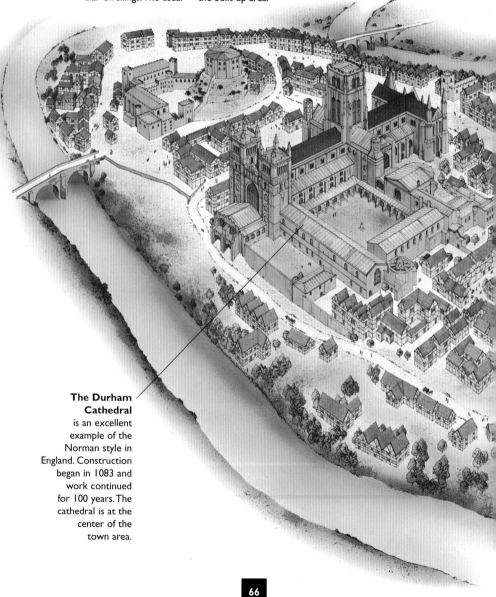

The village
The enormity of the cathedral was pointed up by its position, in the midst of low, irregular dwellings. The usual defensive walls were not needed thanks to the natural defenses provided by the river that completely isolated the built-up area.

The Durham Cathedral
is an excellent example of the Norman style in England. Construction began in 1083 and work continued for 100 years. The cathedral is at the center of the town area.

ROMANESQUE CHURCHES
In the Middle Ages, knowledge of stone-cutting techniques, scaffolding systems, and the laws of statics provided the background for experimentation for all Europe's builders. The Romanesque churches rested on massive pilasters (pillars) that supported semicircular arches, and the roofs were often vaulted.

ple were illiterate, but the sculptures that decorated the facades and the interiors recounted, in images that appealed to the imagination of the viewer, both the truths of the faith and its knowledge and beliefs.

In the past it had been kings, monks, and bishops who constructed the churches; now their builders were the inhabitants of the villages and the cities. What is more, the Romanesque churches became the symbol of a new relationship with religion that first arose in the cities and that grew from an anxiety for renewal. It is therefore no wonder that in the same period, all over Europe, the use of the popular tongue, the language of the people, acquired a certain dignity. Latin, of course, remained the language of tradition. Armies of builders and stonemasons worked throughout Europe to raise the cathedrals, monuments to the spirit of a world that was beginning to demonstrate faith in its own abilities.

URBAN CIVILIZATION
From the ninth through the early fourteenth century, an increase in population and economic resources changed the face of Western Europe. Cities were reborn and trade reopened the West to the rest of the world.

Urban development
The agricultural resources of medieval Europe were sufficient to guarantee population growth and agricultural production capable of sustaining it. The extraordinary conditions linked to the great migrations had, however, hampered such development until the ninth century. Then, after the last of the

invasions, the population began to increase, slowly but constantly. As we saw in the last chapter, the extension of increased arable land, favored by new technology, the availability of manpower, and the efforts of the peasants themselves, had supported and accelerated population growth. The population of Western Europe grew from

One city, many cities
The many cities that developed in the Middle Ages as the population increased had very diverse origins. There were ancient Roman cities like Pavia, Trier, or Paris, new cities founded near monasteries (Malines) or castles (Gand), cities built in hostile but naturally protected environments (Venice), and settlements established for defensive purposes (Avila). Left, a view of medieval Paris in a 16th-century engraving.

about 30 million in the year 1000 to 74 million in 1300. At this point, development ceased. It is thought that no more than 15% of the population of Europe in those times lived in cities, but the very fact that they developed reflected significant changes in European society. Urban centers grew up as marketplaces for farm products that the peasants had begun to produce in excess of their needs. Development of settled areas and markets in turn favored the rise of clearer distinctions between rural and "urban" activities.

Urban life became a driving force in European development and the image of Europe began to assume new aspects that were destined to last.

Urban economy

Manufacturing and commercial activities distinguished the new urban econ-

NEW WALLS
In Florence, one of the richest of the medieval cities, the walls were enlarged a number of times over only 120 years. Few cities were larger: in 1300, London counted 50,000 inhabitants and Paris 200,000.

Roman Florence
In the 3rd century, the population was about 10,000. The city then entered a long period of decline.

The 12th-century walls
In 1050, Florence had 20,000 inhabitants, but by the late 12th century the new walls built in 1175 were already insufficient for the population, then 30,000.

The sixth circle
An ample circle of walls that embraced the new churches of the mendicant friars, built in 1284–1333, proved sufficient until the late 19th century. The population boom that spurred construction of the sixth circle was formidable: 75,000 inhabitants in 1250, 85,000 in 1200 and 100,000 in 1300.

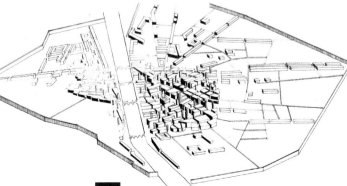

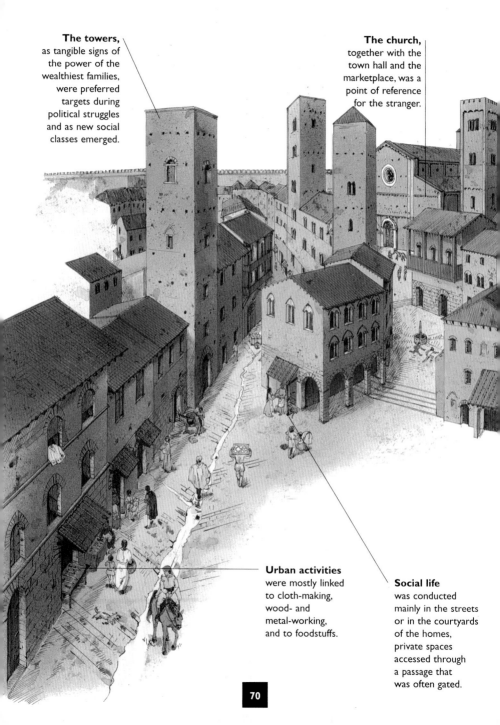

The towers, as tangible signs of the power of the wealthiest families, were preferred targets during political struggles and as new social classes emerged.

The church, together with the town hall and the marketplace, was a point of reference for the stranger.

Urban activities were mostly linked to cloth-making, wood- and metal-working, and to foodstuffs.

Social life was conducted mainly in the streets or in the courtyards of the homes, private spaces accessed through a passage that was often gated.

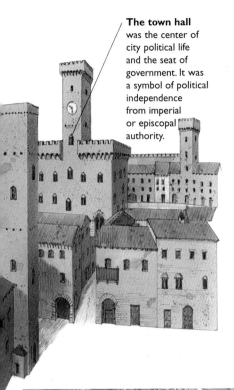

The town hall was the center of city political life and the seat of government. It was a symbol of political independence from imperial or episcopal authority.

Urban topography
Today's cities still reveal their medieval origins in the twisting streets of the historical centers. Above, Cittadella (Padua).

omy. Circulating coin-age was an indispensable requisite for development. The discovery and exploitation of silver deposits in Saxony, Bohemia, Carinthia, Hungary, southern Tuscany in Italy, and in the Pyrenees made coins available from the twelfth century onward. In the mid-1200s, Italian merchants who frequented the ports of the Mediterranean in the areas under Byzantine and Islamic control accumulated gold in payment, and in the second half of the century Florence and Genoa began minting gold coins. Manufacturing industries adopted new organizational and defensive strategies. The major one was the formation of craft corporations or guilds; that is, associations of individuals who performed similar activities and wanted to defend common interests. The guild was an extremely hierarchical body, divided into three categories (masters, journeymen, and apprentices).

Strict regulations and sanctions governed relations between masters and workers, set the duration of apprenticeship, and regulated purchase and use of raw materials. The guild guaranteed the good quality of products. Given the limited market offered by the city, guilds regulated the amount of production and set prices for sales. Uncontrolled competition was not welcome.

Alongside the professional associations political hierarchies also developed, with some overlapping others. The city offered protection and guaranteed the rights of its inhabitants, the

FLANDERS WOOL
One example of specialized production was in the Flanders region, where manufacture of woolen cloth began in the 12th century.

Preparation
The fibers were spun on a spindle until a fine yarn was obtained. In the 13th century, a horizontal frame loom was used for weaving.

Preliminary phases
A bow device was used to separate the fibers of the hand-shorn wool.

Finishing
The woven cloth was fulled (shrunk and matted in water) and the nap was clipped or sheared.

bourgeoisie, and the city people, but political power was in the hands of a few very wealthy families, an aristocratic class whose composition varied from city to city. In many European cities, it was formed mainly of the important merchants. In the communes of north-central Italy, of free landowners, since from the ninth through the eleventh century many rural landowners had "moved to town." These eminent social groups organized communes, associations that grouped together the heads of families of the urban nucleus in order to guarantee order in the city and its independence with respect to the feudal lords. These might be the bishop of a city, the chapter of a cathedral, or the abbot of a monastery. These same social groups dominated the political assembly or council of the city, called *consiglio* in Italian, *rat* in German, and *échevinage* in Flemish.

Thus, toward the end of the eleventh century, cities had begun to obtain a certain degree of independence from the traditional powers in Italy they set out to organize the surrounding territory, later giving rise to city-states of regional dimensions.

In the rest of Europe they rarely succeeded in expanding outside of the confines of the city walls. In Italy, moreover, the contrast between the class of the aristocrats or knights distinguished by a military lifestyle and wealth based in land, and the class of the rich craftsmen and merchants, produced a chronic instability in the city institutions. This was the case in Florence, where the popolo ("people"), a pressure group

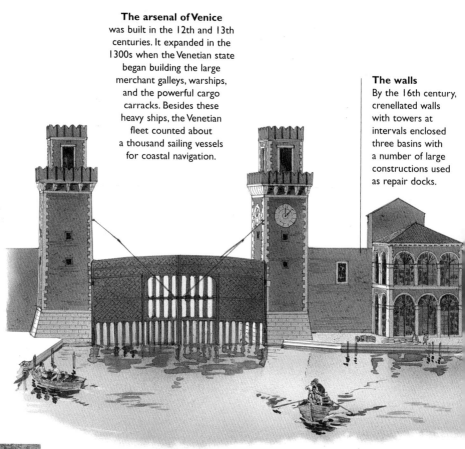

The arsenal of Venice
was built in the 12th and 13th centuries. It expanded in the 1300s when the Venetian state began building the large merchant galleys, warships, and the powerful cargo carracks. Besides these heavy ships, the Venetian fleet counted about a thousand sailing vessels for coastal navigation.

The walls
By the 16th century, crenellated walls with towers at intervals enclosed three basins with a number of large constructions used as repair docks.

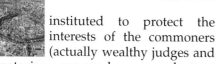 instituted to protect the interests of the commoners (actually wealthy judges and notaries, moneychangers, doctors, spice merchants, wool workers, silk workers, and furriers), took over power in the city, ousting the old nobility once and for all in 1293.

The expansion of trade: the Mediterranean world

Developments in agriculture and increased urbanization were accompanied by a trade revolution. The Mediterranean world became a huge network of sea routes plied by the ships of the Italian maritime republics of Amalfi, Pisa, Genoa, and Venice. The fleets of the Italian cities established contacts with the Byzantine and Muslim powers and, through them, the far-off realms of Asia and Africa. The Genoese, in particular, founded bases on the coast of

The carrack
The Venetian fleet was composed of long-hulled and round-hulled vessels. The latter, called carracks, were used to transport the bulkiest cargos. They had three masts and a high forecastle.

The galley
Venetian galleys defended the large convoys of carracks. They were more graceful and maneuverable, built of quality timber by the skillful craftsmen of the arsenal.

Asia Minor and on the Black Sea. Kaffa on the north shore of the Black Sea and Trebizond on the southern, for example, were the points of arrival of products from the Russian interior and the caravan routes from central Asia. The Venetian ships went to the Near East, to Acre, Jaffa, and Beirut, and then on to Alexandria, which opened the gates to gold-rich Sudan, the Arabian peninsula, and even India. The goods carried by the Italian merchants were generally fabrics, processed luxury items, leathers, spices, dyes, medicinal products, gold, and silver.

The expansion of trade: the northern seas
The other great trade area in Europe was that of the North Sea and Baltic areas, where German merchants held sway. They came to constitute a trading empire, given form in the

Hanseatic League, or Hansa, an organization born in the late 1200s of the fusion of rival associations like those of Cologne, Hamburg, and Lübeck for protection of their common political and economic interests. The Hansa merchants traded mainly in raw materials and foodstuffs; wood for construction, grain, herring, and honey, but also in hides and furs from the north and cloth and woolens from Flanders. The fabrics of Gand, Ypres, and Bruges, famous for their softness, for the perfection of the yarns, and for their splendid colors were also exchanged. The Germans penetrated the Scandinavian area (Stockholm was founded in 1251) and Russia, carrying German colonialism to the east. Through Novgorod, they descended to Kiev.

Shipping costs were high and influenced prices. The price of Russian grain could increase by one-third upon its arrival in France, but triple in Italy.

LÜBECK
The Hanseatic ports, and Lübeck in particular, handled grain from Prussia, furs and honey from Russia, timber for building, tar, dried fish, salted herring, Oriental spices, and the Flanders wools.

The Mediterranean and northern European states traded mainly by sea, and in the various ports of Europe the foreign merchants had warehouses and reception facilities. In general, the merchants of single nations tended to band together in order to better protect their interests. River transport also gave a certain importance: flat-bottomed boats sailed all navigable rivers of Western Europe.

Fairs and markets

European merchants were generally wanderers who went in person to buy or sell goods in far-off places, and never missed an occasion to meet at international fairs. It was not unusual for merchants to form leagues or guilds. The Church learned to appreciate their function as distributors of the well-being of the community-at-large.

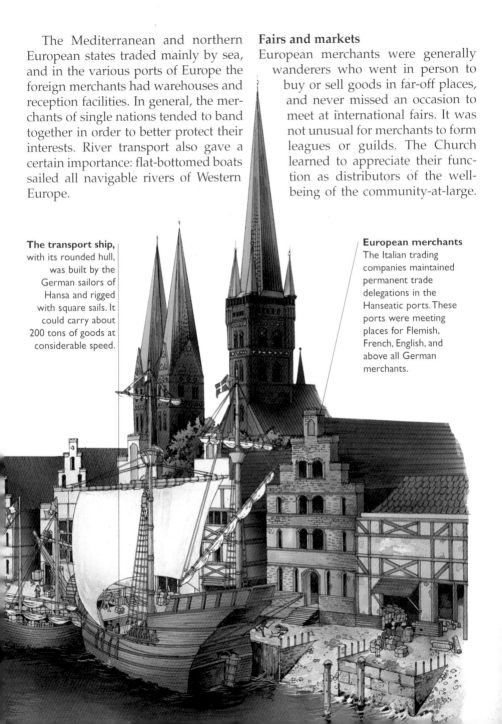

The transport ship, with its rounded hull, was built by the German sailors of Hansa and rigged with square sails. It could carry about 200 tons of goods at considerable speed.

European merchants The Italian trading companies maintained permanent trade delegations in the Hanseatic ports. These ports were meeting places for Flemish, French, English, and above all German merchants.

The bridges
The construction of masonry bridges in place of existing wooden ones was a clear sign of the development of trade and transportation in early Middle Ages.

The cathedral
Construction of Troyes's remarkable Gothic cathedral of Saint-Pierre-et-Saint-Paul began in the late 1200s.

Contracts
Negotiations, payments, and currency exchanges were overseen by fair officials.

THE TROYES FAIR

Between 1150 and the late 1200s, four towns in the Champagne region of France, Bar-sur-Aube, Lagny, Provins, and Troyes, were host to the highest concentration of trade exchanges in all of Europe.

Merchants' lodgings

Foreigners carried on their business in buildings that hosted them. Those who could not find a bed at the fair camped at the edges of the city.

The merchants' wares

The marketplace handled textiles from northern Europe, hides and finished wool cloth, Oriental spices and silks, and horses, all from the south, and furs from Germany in the west.

 It relaxed its opposition to money-lending at interest, which it had always condemned.

At the fairs, merchants found certain guarantees in precise commercial law that targeted maintaining public order and ensuring fair trade. The great fairs of the Champagne region of northern France were important as communication hubs between the north and south of Europe. They differed from local markets, which were held weekly and dealt exclusively in foodstuffs. Fairs were seasonal gatherings that handled all kinds of goods. The Champagne fairs were held six times yearly in four major centers. Thanks to their geographical position they were the prime meeting places for merchants from Flanders, England, Provence, Spain, and Italy. The Christian world, in the twelfth and thirteenth centuries, enjoyed a period of massive economic expansion. This new availability of resources translated into the expansion of a religious-military type, and into strong political upheavals.

The Crusades

In 1096, Pope Urban II (1042–1099) mustered the Christian nobles and knights of Western Europe for a great military undertaking: the liberation of Palestine, the land of the earthly life of Christ that had fallen into Muslim hands in the seventh century. For centuries, Christians made pilgrimages to the Holy Land. And for centuries, they thought that a war against those who were defined as enemies of Christianity was a legitimate project. In a certain sense, the roots of this attitude reached back to the times of the barbarian invasions and the Saxons' forced conversions. More recently, the Europeans had met Muslim invaders in Spain and Sicily, and pirates almost everywhere along the Mediterranean coasts. Therefore there existed all the prerequisites for transforming the traditional religious pilgrimage to the Holy Land into an armed mission.

This new sort of pilgrim, the Crusader, sewed a cross onto his garment. He was a penitent to whom was granted the potential to seek expiation of his sins.

The first Crusaders to go were the poor, peasants whose religious fanaticism caused them to enlist in the project, with little understanding of the consequences of the difficult journey to Jerusalem. In later times Italian ships from Venice and Genoa were launched as much for economic reasons as religious. The next to move were the knights and nobles intent on defending the faith as soldiers of Christ.

The majority of historians count eight official Crusades between 1096 and 1270, but actually their number was infinite, since as soon as one expedition had departed another was immediately recruited. There never were any true interruptions. The Crusades were a failure, for the Christian conquests in the Holy Land could not recruit sufficient men or resources to hold their gain.

The nobles
Urged on by the dream of new conquests and hoping to obtain absolution for their sins, nobles and knights arrived from all parts of the western world.

DEPARTURE FOR THE CRUSADES
In a southern Italian port, a crowd of monks, knights, and the poor await to embark on a Venetian ship.

The religious Crusaders
Inspired by religious sentiment, the Crusaders ousted Greek bishops, estranged from the Church of Rome. Jews they encountered along their way often were pillaged and driven from their homes.

The ships
Most of the ships making up Crusader fleets were supplied by the Republic of Venice.

The poor
Unarmed believers, improvised adventurers, and mad prophets were the advance troops of the First Crusade.

The rebirth of culture

The Europe of the Crusades and urban renewal now began to see another new phenomenon: the rebirth of culture, until that time mainly locked up in monasteries. The first city schools were founded under the aegis of bishops to provide elementary instruction for training new priests and civil servants. Then a new type of higher education took hold, again in the cities, centering on Greek classics and in particular the teachings of Aristotle to explain religious dogmas. In the late eleventh and early twelfth century there were two complementary types of education: the scholastic education of the cities and the monastic education in the abbeys. The university teacher became

THE UNIVERSITY
The culture that was transmitted in the medieval universities was in the main limited to study of the seven liberal arts: the Trivirium, or grammar, rhetoric, and dialectic, and the Quadrivium, or arithmetic, geometry, music, and astronomy. Students graduated in theology, law, and medicine.

The students
were mainly clerics destined to enter the intellectual elite of the Church.

The *laectio* and the *quaestio*
The book played an important role in "scholastic" education. Reading a text was the first phase in the study method (leactio). The second phase consisted of formulating a query (quaestio).

a professional figure licensed and paid by the bishop or by his students. His role became quite prestigious and respected. Students began to move all over Europe to study with different teachers whose authority vested them with the role of leaders—and not only of classes. They even went so far as to fight together with their students against lay power or ecclesiastical authority to defend independent, objective education. This society of students and teachers, which took the name of university, obtained various exemptions and concessions from the municipal or episcopal jurisdictions. They developed self-government, electing a leader, or rector. By the thirteenth century, the university was well on the way to becoming a place where

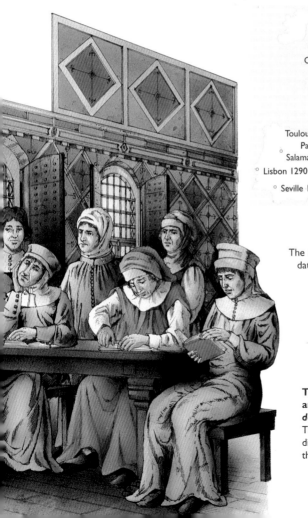

Cambridge 1209
Oxford 1167

Paris 1174
Angers 1229

Montpellier 1289
Toulouse 1229
Palencia 1208
Salamanca 1254
Lisbon 1290
Seville 1254

Padova 1222
Vicenza 1204
Bologna 1158
Arezzo 1215
Naples 1224

The first universities
The map shows the dates of the most famous European universities founded in the 12th and 13th centuries.

The *disputatio* and the *determinatio*
The problem was discussed in the third phase, the disputatio. Its resolution, fruit of an intellectual decision, came in the fourth phase, the determinatio.

students and teachers met in halls and colleges to study the texts of ancient authors and the Bible.

Gothic art

The first schools, as we have said, were founded on the initiative of bishops who resided in the cities. The city church par excellence was the cathedral, the bishop's church. Working together on construction were the architect and the engineer, but also the theologian, who weighed the symbolic significance of every single structural and decorative element. All the city craftsmen took part in the construction of the great cathedrals: carpenters, glass-makers, stonemasons, and many others. The cathedrals were soaring buildings supported by walls laced with multicolored windows under pointed arches. Their bell towers rose to 269 feet (82 m) (Rheims), 426 feet (130 m) (Chartres), 472 feet (144 m) (Strasbourg), and even 525 feet (160 m) (Ulm in southwestern Germany). Gothic art was the triumph of height, of light, of elements that impressed the senses and that expressed human sentiments. It was the art of a young world rich in inventiveness and essentially urban.

The mendicant orders

Another phenomenon that was closely tied to the city was that of the mendicant orders. Like Gothic art, their origins expressed a religious sense that came from below, from the people, from those who actually built the

The Gothic arch is also called the pointed arch, after the form, two arcs that meet at a point. The thrust of the point accentuates the impression that the cathedral is reaching upward to heaven.

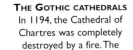

THE GOTHIC CATHEDRALS
In 1194, the Cathedral of
Chartres was completely
destroyed by a fire. The
innovative solutions developed
during the course of its
rebuilding defined the tenets
of Gothic architecture.

Buttresses
are masonry "spurs"
that together with
the external flying
arches took the
lateral thrust of the
roof vaults and the
arches in the interior
of the church.

**Statues as
columns**
The figures that
adorn the
cathedral

are sculpted
directly into
the same
blocks used
as columns.

85

cathedrals. So it was for the Franciscans and the Dominicans, whose religious feeling was rooted in society. In the thirteenth century, the statements of faith were the subject of discussion even in the town square, in the workshops, and at the market. Some preachers, not priests but the sons of craftsmen and tradesmen, spoke of relinquishing wealth in order to recover the true values of the Gospel, of giving up all

The Dominicans
Saint Dominic's mission consisted of preaching from one town or village to another. His order, founded in 1206, soon came to the fore in the fight against heresy and in 1231 was invested by Pope Gregory IX with management of the Inquisition. Right, the pope instituting the Inquisition.

The chapter,
in the monastic communities, was called this because originally every day a monk read a chapter from the Rule to his brethren. The assembly dealt with all the community's problems—both material and spiritual.

THE MENDICANT ORDERS were the Franciscans and the Dominicans, who had felt the winds of reform that began to stir the Church in the 11th century. They renounced all material possessions and lived on charity. Their principal mission was preaching.

types of personal property, of adopting austere customs and plain dress and food, of dedicating their lives to humble work and manual labor. Many among the people heeded their words. St. Francis of Assisi (1182–1226), certainly one of the most important spiritual figures in the history of Christianity, established a small community of brothers who took vows of poverty and preached with no fixed residence. Saint

The rise of the Franciscan Order
The Rule of Saint Francis was given oral approval by Pope Innocent III in 1210. By the early 14th century, the Franciscans probably numbered more than 30,000 men and women.

A TRIAL
At the center of the scene are the Inquisitor and the accused. The aim of the former was to induce him to confess. His guilt may also be proved by testimony given by witnesses.

The accused
One could come under the Inquisition for having listened to heretical speeches or preaching.

Civil authority
Handing over the accused to the civil authorities was tantamount to pronouncing his death sentence.

The Inquisitor
His aim was to convince the accused to confess and return to the straight and narrow path.

Fra' Dolcino
In the winter of 1306–1307, Fra' Dolcino, a heretic whose preaching advocated the abolition of papal power and absolute poverty, stood in armed opposition to ecclesiastical authorities in the Alps in Italy's Piemonte region. He was captured and died under torture in 1307. Above, a miniature from a 14th-century manuscript of Dante's Inferno. Venice, Biblioteca Marciana.

Torture
was authorized by Pope Innocent V in 1252.

 Dominic (1170–1221) founded a community of priests focused on preaching Christian doctrine. The members of both of these brotherly orders were highly educated, but they were also itinerant and poor. They differed from monks who lived in isolation. Franciscans and Dominicans built their churches in the most populous places in the cities. The Franciscans were set apart by their rule of absolute poverty from all other orders. The Dominicans became the champions of the Church's struggle against heresy.

The heretical movements

Not all of those who hoped for Church reform remained faithful to the Orthodox Church. This was the case of the Bogomils. They believed in the existence of two principles, Good (the spirit) and Evil (matter), in perpetual conflict, and therefore refuted the earthly, human aspect of Christ. In the West, another example was offered by the Waldensians (named for Peter Waldo, a rich merchant of Lyon), who rejected the notion of purgatory and certain sacraments like Communion and Confession. Several other sects grew up beginning in the eleventh century, and drew their strength mainly from the people, and also demanded reform of Church authorities. As they became more combative and more popular, the Church hierarchy declared them heretics; that is, dissenters from official Church dogma. Systematic repression started in the

THE BLACK DEATH
The plague reached Europe in
the mid-1300s when Genoese
ships arrived from a Black Sea
trading post carrying infected
persons and stowaway rats.

Macabre scenes
Wars, fires, and
epidemics made
life difficult during
the Middle Ages.
Death is one of
the most often
represented
subjects in the
art of the times.

Rats
The culprit in the
spread of the
plague bacillus
was the rat flea.

early thirteenth century;
Pope Innocent III (1198–1216)
proclaimed the Albigensian
Crusade against the Albigensian
heretics. Another weapon used against
heresy was the Inquisition; that is, systematic ferreting out of heretic doc-
trines through investigations, question-
ing, and trial before a tribunal. Actual
sentencing and punishment were delegated to the civil authorities.

The population crash

The period spanning the eleventh
and thirteenth centuries was, for the
Christian West, a time of expansion and
political reorganization. Nevertheless,
by the first years of the fourteenth century, many regions of Europe were
more populous than the agricultural
resources of the age were capable of
supporting. Famine again afflicted the
population and reduced people's resis-

Divine punishment
In the Middle Ages, it was believed that the plague was a punishment sent by God, and for this reason processions of penitents, so-called flagellants, walked the roads scourging their bodies as a sign of penitence.

Assistance
was supplied above all by the religious orders, but medical knowledge was scarce. The dead were burned or buried in common graves.

tance to disease. Medicine was still a backward science, if a science at all. Public hygiene was virtually unheard of, and overcrowding in the cities had increased the probability of epidemic. By the thirteenth–fourteenth century, population growth had come to a standstill. But the hardest blow was inflicted by the appalling Black Death that spread through Europe between 1347 and 1351. From then on, the plague presented itself at intervals to afflict different areas of Europe.

Halfway through the 1400s, the population of Europe was less than half of what it had been at the beginning of the previous century, and a new page of economic and political history was about to begin.

EMPIRES AND SOVEREIGN STATES

With the failure of the project that aimed at creating a universal empire in Europe, Italy and Germany remained politically fragmented, while great territorial states such as England, France, and Spain began to form.

Pope and emperor

In Byzantium, the problem of relations between empire and church had for some time ceased to exist, since the emperor had become the repository of many spiritual and temporal powers. In the West, instead, the problem had emerged with Charlemagne, in the ninth century. Faced with a society that had bowed to corruption and immorality and had yet to recover from the torment of the barbarian migrations and the violence that had followed, the Frankish king, as emperor, also felt the need to reform the Church. The reform soon turned to control. Charlemagne began to appoint bishops himself. This power of appointment, known as

INVESTITURE
is the attribution of a power by the bestowal of his office from a lay person to a bishop. With time, this type of power was likened to a true feudal benefice and, as such, became subject to a ritual ceremony.

The empire in 1050
In the mid-11th century, the center of the Holy Roman Empire was in what are today Germany and Austria, with territories stretching from Burgundy in France to today's Hungary and northern Italy.

investiture, had been transferred down through the hierarchy of feudal society to the smallest vassals. Every prince felt himself empowered to appoint his own bishop, who promised loyalty in exchange for a fief. The Holy Roman Emperor, Otto I, made the control and protection yet more strict. The bishops he himself had appointed and invested with fiefs were the administrators of his empire; the Privilegium Othonis of 962 made the very election of the pope subject to his approval. To this state of affairs, the Church had countered with the Gregorian Reform, which takes its name from Pope Gregory VII (1073–1085). The pope issued 27 articles, the *Dictatus papae,* in which he confirmed the absolute power of the pope over the entire Church and the superi-

The emperor
The support of the bishops was important for the emperor. When the investiture conflict (1073–1122) ended, spiritual power went to the bishops and the pope, temporal power to the emperor.

The bishop, head of the local church, was caught up in the feudal mechanism when his appointment came to depend on a nonreli-gious authority. As a vassal of the king and in turn a lord over other vassals, the bishop acted like any other feudal lord.

The pastoral staff
From the emperor, the bishop received the pastoral staff or crosier, symbol of episcopal power.

ority of the Church over any temporal power. The pope had turned the tables: now he held the power to depose emperors. They reached a compromise in 1122 with the Concordant of Worms, by which the emperor agreed to renounce investiture of the bishops but retained the right to veto the Church's candidates. This was the first concrete acknowledgment by the empire of the separation of spiritual and temporal powers.

The breakup of the empire

In the late twelfth century, even though the investiture controversy had practically ended, the dispute between church and empire for control of the Christian world was still an open question. It was destined to have especially negative consequences for Germany and Italy. These conflicts worked in favor of those who wanted to weaken the unity of the empire and contributed to the political breakup that endured until the nineteenth century.

In Germany, the struggle between the papacy and the empire reinforced the rival princes, enemies of the emperor. Moreover, the emperors were often called to Italy and were forced to ignore German affairs for long periods. On the other hand, it was in their best interests to court Italy. By demanding payment of the taxes due to the emperor, who was also king of Italy although his kingdom extended only as far as the Po Valley, they hoped to profit by the extraordinary economic progress of northern Italy. Here they came into

THE BATTLE OF LEGNANO
Emperor Frederick I Barbarossa was defeated in 1176 at Legnano in northern Italy by a coalition of the communes of the Lombard cities. This episode put an end to the emperor's plans to install an imperial government on the Italian peninsula, under his rule.

The carroccio
was a large wheeled vehicle used in battle in the 12th and 13th centuries as a symbol of the common defense mounted by citizens. When the free cities began enlisting mercenary soldiers, ostentation of this symbol became senseless. Mass was celebrated on the carroccio and from it the military leader commanded his troops.

The standards
were painted in strong colors or covered in multicolored cloth. At Legnano, the standard of Milan, which led the expedition, was at the top of a pole.

conflict with the spirit of independence of the Italian city-states. The long reign of Frederick I Barbarossa (1152–1190) was the moment of greatest splendor of imperial power in Germany. His son Henry VI (1165–1197) succeeded in winning, by marriage, the crown of the Norman kingdom of Sicily, which he left to his son Frederick II.

Frederick II of Swabia (1194–1250) thus found himself reigning over both Germany and the state created by the Normans in southern Italy, the kingdom of Sicily, where Greek, Arabic, and Latin cultures intermingled. The Norman state had been perturbed before his coming of age by the behavior of the feudal lords, who had appropriated rights and taxes but had not succeeded in destroying the basic unity of the state. Frederick II created a centralized government, imposed a strict tax collection policy, had the feudal castles torn down, and instituted a royal army. In northern Italy, he fought bitterly against the communes, which did not acknowledge his imperial authority.

In 1220, after the death of Pope Innocent III (1198–1216), who had worked actively to keep the empire and the kingdom of Sicily separate, Frederick II had himself proclaimed emperor. In Italy, instead, the struggle between church and empire created factions within the cities between the supporters of the emperor vs. those who instead supported papal policy. At the same

FALCONRY
Frederick II loved hunting, and preferred using leopards or hunting with falcons. But he also loved the natural sciences, and was a scholar of the behavior of falcons and their prey.

Castel del Monte (Puglia, Italy)
Begun in 1240, this massive Gothic castle is a synthesis of the culture of the emperor and his interest in the classical world, relations with the Cistercian milieu, and familiarity with the technical knowledge of Islamic civilization.

Falcons
Scores of falconers cared for the falcons. Frederick II kept up a lively correspondence on the subject with Arab sovereigns.

Frederick II
was the last of
the great medieval
emperors and
the first modern
statesman. His
mother was

Constance of
Altavilla, daughter
of Roger II, the
founder of the
Norman monarchy
in southern Italy.

time it favored the political ascendency of the rival free cities and therefore hindered political unification of the peninsula. Italy at the time of Frederick II was divided into three parts. The north was the realm of the German emperors, but the cities demanded greater independence—and the star of the Republic of Venice was rising. Central Italy was the Patrimony of Saint Peter, a territory in which the popes had reigned supreme as temporal rulers since the eighth century. In the south, Frederick II ruled over what had once been a Norman kingdom.

The court
Frederick II was famous as a man of culture. He spoke Arabic and wrote a treatise on falconry entitled On the Art of Hunting with Birds.

The Saxon formation
The king's nobles were arrayed along the crest and the infantry on the flanks, in such a manner as to form a wall of shields and lances 10 to 12 lines deep.

England

While in Italy and Germany the central authority of the monarchy was opposed by the city-states, by the pope, and by the old feudal princes, the opposite phenomenon was occurring in the western portion of Christian Europe. England, as had long been the case in southern Italy, was ruled by a Norman dynasty. William the Conqueror (1022–1066) had taken the throne by force, defeating Saxon King Harold II (1022–1066) at the Battle of Hastings, and installed the Norman aristocracy in the new kingdom. This had permitted William to act in three essential ways. First of all, he acted to preserve and strengthen royal rights in regard to the legal, administrative, and financial systems inherited from the previous dynasty. Secondly, he sought to install in England the complicated system of feudal relationships that bound the king and his vassals, all to the benefit of the Norman nobles. Thirdly, he was able to organize his

realm on solid social and material foundations, thanks in part to a general survey of men, lands, and the incomes of the landholders of the island—the Domesday Book. Through this information the king was informed of the economic capacities of his subjects for taxation purposes, and began to keep confiscated lands for himself, thus creating a vast holding of crown lands.

The English crown, in the beginning very strong, slowly weakened. William's successors started a civil war that last-ed for some twenty years (1135–1154) and ended only when Henry II Plantagenet ascended the throne. Henry II governed over a territory comprising England and about half of France. It later contributed to sparking the long struggle between French and English for the throne of France: the Hundred Years' War. Henry organized his state, but in doing so ran afoul of the powerful Church, whose support had been enlisted by the early kings against the many enemies that threatened the crown. A crusade launched by Richard the Lion-Hearted, son of Henry II, had drained the coffers of the state and the wars against the Scots and the French had further weakened the monarchy to the advantage of the Church and the feudal barons. The result of all this was the concession, in 1215, of the Magna Carta, by which the king confirmed the rights and the liberties of the English aristocracy, of the churches, and of the cities in relation to the crown. It set precise limits on the power wielded by the king, subject from then on to obtaining the consent of the aristocracy and later of the minor nobility and the middle class. The Magna Carta should be seen less as the capitulation of the monarchy than as the first step in the direction of the birth of Parliament.

France

Since 987, the crown of France had been in the hands of the Capetian dynasty, which was destined to reign for eight centuries, first directly and then through collateral lines. It was a feudal monarchy founded on bonds of fealty between the rulers of the principalities and the king.

The question of investiture was decided under King Philip I (1052–1108). The agreement with the papacy and the high clergy, the central position of the Capetian dominions with respect to the other French principalities, and the luck of having an unbroken line of male descendants—which assured the continuation of the dynasty and obviated questions

THE MAGNA CARTA
Among other principles, the Magna Carta, drawn up in 63 articles, stated the abolition of arbitrary arrest and that "no free man shall be imprisoned or disseised [dispossessed] except by the lawful judgment of his peers or by the law of the land." Although the form has changed with time, the right of habeas corpus is still in force today.

King John (1199–1216)
signed the Magna Carta, which on the one hand guaranteed that the king's officials would not abuse the barons, and on the other, sanctioned the existence of these officials.

Murder in the cathedral
Intent on curbing the privileges enjoyed by the Church, Henry II came into conflict with the Archbishop of Canterbury Thomas Becket (1118–1170), who was later murdered in the cathedral, perhaps at instigation of the king himself. Becket was canonized in 1173.

THE KING'S TOUCH
People had attributed to the
king of France the power to
heal, by the laying on of his hands,
an inflammation of the lymphatic
system called scrofula caused
by the tuberculosis bacillus.

THE HUNDRED YEARS' WAR,
begun in 1337, pitted the crowns of
France and England against each other
for possession of the throne of France.
This engagement between the two most
powerful kingdoms in Europe ended in
1453 with the removal of the English
from French territory and confirmation
of France as a compact territorial state.
Above, Joan of Arc, heroine of France's
struggle against the English.

Horror
Scrofula enlarges
the lymph glands of the
neck, causing horrible
disfigurement of the face.

of succession to the throne —were the principal reasons for its longevity.

Especially during the reign of Louis VI (1108–1137), the alliance with the Church reinforced the idea that kings had a healing power. It was believed that kings were capable of miraculous healing and thus invested with authority by God himself. Louis VI spent the years of his reign attempting to impose his authority over the small barons of the Ile-de-France. Philippe Augustus (1180–1223) was the real founder of French kingship. He imposed monarchy in the realm. The crucial moment was the conquest of Normandy from the English in 1204. During the struggle against the Albigensian heretics (1209–1229), the people of Languedoc in southern France were also made the king's subjects all the way to the Loire Valley.

The progressive expansion of the kingdom led Louis IX (1214–1270) to

The basin
After having touched the sick person, the king washed his hands in a basin. The water was then considered to possess miraculous properties.

Louis IX
was canonized in 1289 by Pope Boniface VIII because of his moral and religious virtues.

create a bureaucracy that gradually took over territorial administration. It was composed of nobles and common citizens and marked a decisive step in the evolution of the feudal monarchy away from the old network of bonds of vassallage.

Spain

The Iberian peninsula was colonized in the fifth century by the Visigoths, whose political system had been weak-ened by the practice of dividing the kingdom among the heirs of the rulers. Nevertheless, what most indelibly marked the area of Spain was the arrival of the Arabs and Berbers in the eighth century. The Muslim conquest gave rise to a political structure, with its capital at Córdoba, which however never succeeded in embracing the entire peninsula. A strip of territory in the northwest remained under the con-trol of several small Christian king-

Valencia
In 1094, after some years of siege, El Cid succeeded in taking over the emirate of Valencia. In 1099, the Moors laid siege to the city of Valencia, in the hopes of winning back their capital.

The body of El Cid
During a skirmish, El Cid was mortally wounded. The Moors were certain he was dead. To rally troop morale, his companions tied his body to his saddle.

El Cid's ghost
The appearance of El Cid's mounted body on the battlefield struck panic among the Moors, who fled from what they believed was the ghost of the hero.

EL CID CAMPEADOR
is the legendary name of the 9th-century Castilian warrior Rodrigo Diaz de Vivar. Although well-known as a Christian hero who opposed the Moors and a model of chivalrous virtue, the figure of El Cid is nevertheless shrouded in mystery. His exploits are the subject of many heroic poems and romantic epics in Spanish literature.

doms. In the ninth century, the most powerful of these kingdoms was Navarre, governed by Sancho III the Great who later gained control over much of Christian Spain. When he died in 1054, his kingdom was divided among his sons. Of these Christian states, Leon-Castile became the strongest, together with Aragon, the leader of the Reconquista against the Moors, the name Spaniards gave to the Muslims. Castile, at one point, controlled more than half of the Iberian peninsula and was transformed into a true monarchy by Alfonso X (1252–1284). Aragon, which had centered its power in the south, became a great and long-lasting maritime power. Other states were formed as the Reconquista proceeded; Portugal became independent from 1139. The Reconquista concluded only in 1492, when the last of the Muslim kingdoms fell.

Al-Andalus, or Arab Spain, was a renowned center of material culture, artistic and intellectual activity, and philosophy and science, especially between the tenth and the thirteenth centuries. During the same period, from the political point of view, it was often fragmented into small local kingdoms and the dominion of the Muslim dynasties of Africa. From the tenth century onward they began sending aid to their European sister states as the latter were attacked by the Christians.

TOWARD WORLD POLITICS

The autumn of the era of the Middle Ages saw conflicts in the Muslim world, Sub-Saharan Africa, and China. Thanks to intensified trade and, later, the era of the great discoveries, the world became more closely knit.

The crisis in the Byzantine Empire

In the late eleventh century, Constantinople was a splendid metropolis of about one-half million inhabitants (Rome, at the time, counted less than 30,000), a crossroads for men and goods at the fulcrum of Europe, Asia, and Africa. It was impregnable, defended on the one side by the sea and on the land side by its circle of walls. Huns, Avars, Bulgarians, and Arabs had tried to take the city, all in vain. The emperors had always repulsed the invaders, but they were unable to prevent disruptive internal factors from arising. The strong points of the Byzantine state, which had always been a large fleet and a sizeable class of peasant-

THE BYZANTINE LITURGY
is a triumph of color
and light. Christ is
represented triumphant.

The Patriarch of Constantinople
was the head of the
Byzantine Church,
second in the empire
only to the emperor.
In the 10th century
he led a Church made
up of 57 metropolitans,
49 archbishoprics, and
514 bishops' sees.

Monasticism
In the Byzantine world, the monasteries were places of prayer and asceticism but also possessed great authority and many privileges. For example, they paid no taxes to the emperor. The most famous monastic community was founded in the 10th century on Mount Athos in Greece.

warriors ready to defend their lands, began to weaken about the year 1000. From then on, the majority of troops were mercenaries (often Seljuqs, Turks, or Normans) and this fact earned the Byzantines the disdain of the West, where the ideal of the knight as defender of the weak was very much alive. What is more, many key functions in the government of the empire (in which the only hereditary office had until then been that of the emperor himself) had been monopolized and then made hereditary by a few wealthy families. To complete the picture, in 1054 an effort to solve differences between the Orthodox and Catholic Church practices had ended in failure.

The passage of western Crusader troops heading for the Holy Land also created problems for the Byzantine emperors. It was a cause for tension

Byzantine priests were not required to remain celibate, but the bishops, who were monks, could not marry.

The iconostasis of the Byzantine Church separates the clergy from ordinary people and is richly decorated with sacred images called icons.

between Byzantium and Europe's powerful feudal lords, who had no intention of swearing allegiance to the emperor nor of relinquishing to the Greeks the lands they had conquered. In 1204, a Crusader army backed by the Venetians laid siege to Constantinople as it was heading for the Holy Land. The great city fell and a Latin empire, which lasted until 1261, was established in Constantinople.

The Ottoman Empire

In the thirteenth century, the balance of power in the Islamic world, in its eastern portion, was upset by a new group of Mongol invaders. In 1258, the Mongol invaders conquered Baghdad, putting an end to the centuries-old Abbasid caliphate. After a while some converted to Islam and were assimilated into Muslim society, which in the meantime had greatly changed. The abandonment of the irrigation works and the opening of new trade routes had by this time meant the decline of Iraq. The real centers of Muslim civilization had moved east into Persia, or toward the Nile Valley. The Muslim East, with Persian mediation, gave rise to a splendid flowering of the arts of poetry, architecture, and painted miniatures. The western portion of the area preserved the more distinctively Arabic of the legal, literary, and mystic traditions. The Mongol invaders fused with the Seljuq sultanate that had ruled since the eleventh century in Iraq.

From Anatolia, known today as Turkey, a number of small principali-

THE OTTOMAN STATE
From a single principality, in the late 13th century the Ottomans expanded to the detriment of the Byzantine Empire, thanks to their well-organized army.

Turks and Mongols originated in the same regions and used similar military tactics and weapons. Mounted archers were a Mongol tradition.

The janissaries were members of an elite Ottoman infantry corps founded in the late 14th century, recruited from among Christian youths taken from their families and educated according to Islamic principles.

ties put pressure on the Byzantine Empire. One of these territories was governed by the Ottomans, who by the end of the 1300s had secured control of all of Anatolia and the Balkans. In 1453 the Ottomans would conquer Constantinople.

The Mongols

The Mongols were nomadic people of the Asian steppes, speaking a language similar to Turkish. Their conquests played out in four phases. The first was that led by Genghis Khan (1167–1227), who extended his empire from Beijing in China to the Volga River in Russia. The second was conducted by Genghis's son Ogadai (1185–1241), who penetrated as far as Poland but failed to conquer it. The third was led by Kublai Khan (1214–1294), who completed the conquest of China, and by his brother Hulagu Khan (1217–1265), who in 1258 destroyed Baghdad, the capital of the Abbasid Empire.

Hulagu Khan marched into Damascus in 1260, but the Mamluk sultan of Egypt, Baybars I, returned in time from Cairo and forced him to retreat. The last assault was staged by the Turkic warrior Timur the Lame. The dominion of the Mongols, expert horsemen, ferocious warriors, disciplined and well-coordinated fighters, was relatively brief. Following their conquests, they were unable to create an original and lasting civilization. Rather, they marked the end of an era. Since the dawn of civilization, the farming populations had always lived under the threat of incursions by the nomads, whose lifestyle both demanded and aided them in developing great physical prowess. However, the invention of

Genghis Khan gathered together the various Mongol clans and set out in 1211 to conquer a vast empire.

gunpowder and firearms came about at the same time as the last Mongol invasions, and from that time onward the battles were no longer decided by sheer force. During the centuries that followed, Russia and China, the two states hardest hit by invasions of nomadic peoples, succeeded in stopping the warlike nomads of the steppes once and for all.

China

We left China in the ninth century, under the Tang dynasty, which had created political unity and general well-being in the country. In 906, the Tang dynasty fell and China broke into ten regional states, to be reunified only between 960 and 979 under the Song dynasty. The Songs had lost some former territories, and their state was less well organized than

A MONGOL CAMP
The Mongol army was fearsome, with its efficient cavalry, inured to fatigue and very well-disciplined. There were many Turks among its ranks.

Expert horsemen
The Mongols rode small, fast horses with great stamina. The horsemen covered long distances with dried meat as their only food.

Kublai Khan (1214–1294) the grandson of Genghis Khan, was the founder of the Mongol Yüan dynasty that reigned in China from 1260 through 1368.

Marco Polo (1254–1324), born in Venice of a family of merchants and travelers, recounted his twenty years of travels in Asia in the celebrated book Il Milione (Travels of Marco Polo).

that of the Tangs, more suspicious of foreigners, and weakened by internal struggles. From 1127 through 1279, following the invasion of northern China by the Jurchens, the Songs reigned only over the central and southern portions of the land, but despite this the economy continued to prosper and between 750 and 1000 the Chinese population doubled, reaching about 100 million. The Song capital, Kaifeus, was the world's largest metropolis at the time. The figurative arts, literature, philosophy, science, and technology achieved exceptional levels of excellence. Literacy increased, thanks in part to the invention of printing (although not in movable type as was to

The Court
The imperial palace was crowded with officers and knights, provincial governors, army officials, astronomers and astrologers, falcon masters, and the ambassadors of far-off realms.

happen in Europe in the fifteenth century, given the enormous number of Chinese ideograms) in the form of transfers from woodcuts. In the largest cities, a wealthy and cultured middle class patronized the popular theater and short-story writing. Civil service recruitment examinations guaranteed that the state was administered not by the aristocracy but by competent career bureaucrats. Many merchants became extremely wealthy; in response to their needs a complex financial system emerged that made use of banks, credit instruments, and printed paper money. Large properties were consolidated in the rural areas and were farmed by tenants and day-laborers.

The Mongol invasion of 1215 placed the Yüan dynasty on the throne. For China, with its traditionally agricultural and sedentary civilization, the reign of the mounted nomads was a traumatic period. Canals, dikes, roads, and bridges fell into disrepair. Only in 1368, with the rise to power of the Ming dynasty, did the country recover. Certainly, the Mongol reign in China was a time of calm for the rest of the Eurasian world. This was, in fact, the period during which contacts and caravan expeditions between the West and the East recommenced.

Muslim and Sub-Saharan Africa

From the earliest times, northern Africa

TIMBUKTU
was the capital of Mali, one of the most extensive and richest of the African empires in the 13th–16th centuries. It was a center of culture and commerce that welcomed caravans carrying copper, salt, and manufactured goods that were traded with powdered gold. Africa was the major supplier to the Mediterranean countries prior to the discovery of the Americas.

The homes
The most important homes were square in form with a terraced roof.

had been included in the circuit of Mediterranean trade and cultural exchanges. This was not true for Africa south of the Sahara. The desert had always constituted a barrier, an ocean of sand, between the Mediterranean world and the rest of Africa. Between 900 and 1500, Egypt was governed by Muslim dynasties: the Fatimids, the Ayyubids, and Mamluks. They were energetic traders in an area embracing the Red Sea and the Arabian Sea areas, and laid a base for the rejuvenation of the old Ethiopian Empire.

By the year 1000 the Maghreb (north-western Africa) had been Islamic for more than three centuries and was the seat of the great Almoravid and the Almohad Berber empires.

From 1000 to 1500, Islam spread into the African interior up the course of the Nile to the Christian kingdoms of

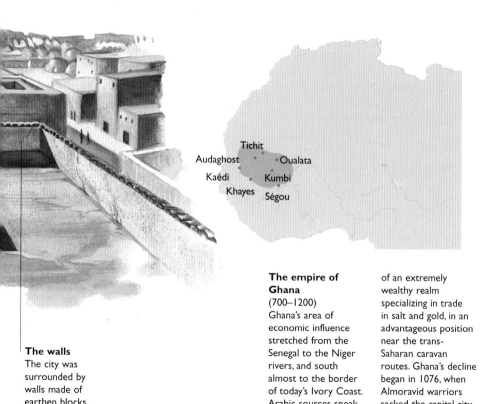

The walls
The city was surrounded by walls made of earthen blocks.

The empire of Ghana
(700–1200)
Ghana's area of economic influence stretched from the Senegal to the Niger rivers, and south almost to the border of today's Ivory Coast. Arabic sources speak of an extremely wealthy realm specializing in trade in salt and gold, in an advantageous position near the trans-Saharan caravan routes. Ghana's decline began in 1076, when Almoravid warriors sacked the capital city.

Nubia, along the coasts of the Horn of Africa (facing southern Arabia), and across the Sahara into the Sudan from the Nile to the Senegal River. The Muslims crossed the Sahara as merchants or travelers, moving from one oasis to the next. They exchanged salt and luxury items (and later firearms) for gold and, above all, slaves. Since the eighth century the economies of the Middle East and Christian Europe depended on African gold.

This growth in trade favored the rise of various states in the Sudan. Two of the largest were Ghana, which flourished between the eighth and the eleventh century, and Mali, which reached the height of its splendor in the fourteenth century. While Europe was suffering a period of decline due to the plague and the Hundred Years' War between France and England, certain of the African kingdoms were famous, above all in the Muslim world, for their walled cities full of marvels. The universities of Timbuktu and Djenné attracted many scholars and poets. In general, the Africa in which the Europeans had yet to arrive included some very large states. The dominion of the kings over these territories was supported by a combination of military might and diplomatic alliances with local princes. The royal judges administered justice and a class of bureaucrats collected taxes and regulated commerce. The tendency in these states, whose borders were generally ill-defined, was to develop toward the interior of the continent rather than toward the coast.

The market, in the separatist Ismaili communities, was not located alongside the mosque in the traditional way, since it was the site of contacts with the merchants, who were foreigners to the community.

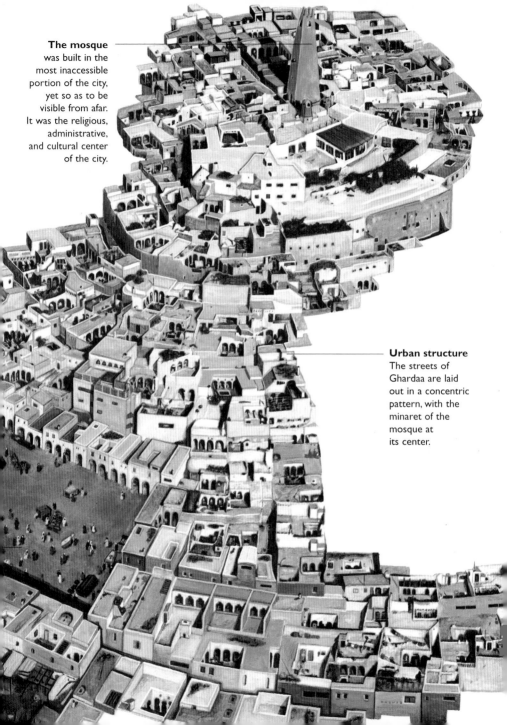

The mosque was built in the most inaccessible portion of the city, yet so as to be visible from afar. It was the religious, administrative, and cultural center of the city.

Urban structure
The streets of Ghardaa are laid out in a concentric pattern, with the minaret of the mosque at its center.

Toward the modern era

Starting in the early fifteenth century, the Portuguese expanded toward Africa. The end of Mongol domination in Asia, which had brought relative peace, and the advance of the Turks at the expense of the Byzantine Empire caused the caravan routes to the Orient to be interrupted and broke the West's hold over the eastern Mediterranean. In 1453, Constantinople was conquered by the Ottoman sultan Mehmed II (145–1481). The Eastern Roman Empire, over a thousand years old but by this time tiny and entirely Greek-speaking, ceased to exist. Many Greeks fled to Italy, where they contributed, in the fifteenth centu-

The Ottoman fleet
In order to enter the Golden Horn, the Turks carried their ships over the Pera peninsula on rollers made of tree trunks, since the strait was closed off by an enormous chain stretching from one side to the other.

THE FALL OF CONSTANTINOPLE
On May 29, 1453, Ottoman troops commanded by Mehmed II (ca. 1432–1481) entered Constantinople, which they sacked and plundered for three days.

ry, to the birth of Renaissance civilization. The Portuguese went looking for a sea route to the Orient and circumnavigated Africa in search of gold, spices, and slaves. The same motivation underlay Spain's decision to grant backing and financing for Christopher Columbus's project to sail west to reach the Orient.

The initiatives by the Spaniards and the Portuguese, and soon by the explorers of other European nations as well, with France and England in the lead, were destined to link old and new continents in an increasingly global economy.

The modern era was in the making.

The cannon
Powerful siege artillery permitted the Turks to breach the city walls.

Index

The numbers in *italics* refer to items discussed in the captions.

A
Aachen (*Acquisgranum*) 29, *29*
   Palatine Chapel *29*
   Cathedral *29*
   Roman spa 29
Abbasid Empire 20, *22*, 110
Abbasids 23, *23*, 108
Abbeys 30, 58, 84
   Benedictine *24*
   Corbie 58
   Montecassino *24*
   Cistercian 61–62, *61*
   Citeaux *62*
   Sénanque *61*
   Cluniac 61–62
   of Cluny *58–59*, *60*, 61
Abd-ar-Rahaman *26*
Abraham 22
Acre 75
Afghanistan
   Chinese conquests 20
Africa 115–118
   architecture *114–115*, *116–117*
   Fatimid kingdoms 23
   homes *114*
   Islamic domination *30*, 105, 116, *116–117*
   occupation by Vandals *10*
   Portuguese domination 118
   trade 6, 75, *114–116*
   Vandal kingdom 13
Agriculture 4, 7, 8, 11, 26, 40–41, 42–48, 52–54, 56, 68–69, 74
   breaking and tilling of land 43, 46, 52–54, 62
   technical innovations 40–43, *42–43*, 68
Al-Andalus 105
Al-Mansur 22
Alani *10–11*
Albigensian heretics 89, 90, 102
Alemanni 8
Alexander the Great 4, 17
Alexandria, of Egypt 75
Alfonso X 105
Almohad Empire 116
Almoravid Empire *115*, 116
Amalfi 75
America
   Viking settlements 32
Anatolia
   Ottoman domination *108–109*, 109

Angles 8, *10*
Antioch 26
Apprentices 71
Arabian peninsula
   Bedouin settlements 20
   trade with Venice 75
Arab 20–24, 31, *31*, 80 *see also* Islam
   cities *116–117*
   crafts 4, *22*
   language 22–24, 96
   science and technology 24
   trade 75
Aragon, kingdom of 105
Archers *99*, *108*
Arches *see also* Architecture
   pointed or Gothic *84*, *85*, 86
   rounded *67*
Architecture *13*, *46–47*, 84–86, *85*
   Romanesque *66–67*
Aristotle 24, 83
Arsacid dynasty 17
Asia Minor 4
Asia
   Chinese conquests 19
   invasion by Huns 11
   nomad peoples *10*
   trade with Italy 75
Attila 12
Austrasia, kingdom of 27
Avars 106
Avila *68*
B
Baghdad 20, *22–23*, *23*, 108, 110
Balearic Islands 33
Baltic Sea, trade on 76
Bar-sur-Aube *79*
Bavarians 8
Baybars I 110
Bedouins 20
Beggars *80*, 82
Beijing 110
Beirut 75
Bishops 26, 58, 67, 73, 83, 84, *88*, 92, 93, *93*
   Byzantine *107*
   counts 93
   as imperial officers 39
   of Macon 61
Bogomils 89
Bohemia, Duchy of 38
Boniface VIII, Pope *103*
Bourgeoisie 73, 74, 100

Bourgogne 35
Bow and arrow—use by Central Asian nomads 11
Britain
   Roman domination 4
   occupation by Jutes, Angles, and Saxons *10*
British Isles 29
Britons *10*
Bruges 76
Buddhism 19–20, *19*
   Temple of Todjai *19*
Bulgarians 36, 38, 106
Burgundians 11
Byelorussians 36
Byzantine Empire *see* Empire, Eastern Roman
Byzantium *see* Constantinople
C
Cadiz 33
Cairo 23
Capetian dynasty 100–102
Carolingian Empire *see* Holy Roman Empire
Carolingians 27, 29–30, 45, 103
Carpaccio, Vittore *75*
Carroccio *95*
Castel del Monte *96*
Castles 35, 43, 46, *46–47*, *48–49*, 49, 51, *56*, 67, *68*
   architecture *46–47*
   Tyrol Castle *46–47*
Catalonia 33
Champagne fairs 79–80, *79*
Chapter, monastic assembly *86*
Charlemagne 29–30, *29*, *32*, 38, *39*, 92
Charles Martel *26*, 27
Chartres, cathedral of *84–85*, 86
China 18–20, *18*, *19*, *35*, 111–114
   art 112–113
   civil wars 19
   crafts 20
   economy 112
   Great Wall 19
   invasion by Huns *11*, 12, 19
   invasion by Mongols 110, 114
   language 20, 113
   organization of society 113
   population 112
   religion 20
   science and technology 113
   trade 20

Christianity 5–7, 12, 14, 22, 24–29, 33, 35–36, 37, 52–53, 64–65, 65, 84, 86–90
  Arian rite 14
  in societal organization 39
  Church 52, 52, 57, 61, 67, 79, 86, 92–94, 100, 102
  Eastern 7, 26, 36, 38, 81, 106–107, 107
  Patriarch 14, 106
  organization 26
  privileges 101
  reform 62, 86, 89–90, 92
  Western (Latin) 7, 26, 38, 58–64, 80, 91, 107
Cistercians see Orders, Monastic
Cities
  African 114–117, 116
  European
    economy 42, 69, 71-74
    population 42, 68–69, 69, 91
    social organization 70-71, 74
    urban development 56, 56–57, 66–71, 67
  Islamic 22, 24
Cittadella (Padua, Italy) 71
City Councils 73
Clerics 82, 87
Clovis I 10, 27
Cluniac monks see Orders, Monastic
Coins 54, 71, 114
  Byzantine 24
  gold coins 71
  Muslim 24
Columbus, Christopher 119
Communes 71, 73, 74, 94, 95, 96, 100
  Milan 95
Communication routes 32, 63
  Roman 4, 98
Constance of Altavilla 97
Constantine 7, 39
Constantinople 7, 14–15, 15, 20, 22, 36, 108, 118, 118
  Church of Hagia Sofia 15
Copyists 26
Córdoba 23, 105
Corinth 26
Corpus Juris Civilis 16
Corsica 31
Corvées 54
Counts 29, 45
Crafts guilds 71, 73, 74
  apprenticeship 71
Croatians 36, 38

Crop rotation 41, 43
Crusades 51, 53, 80–83, 90, 100, 108
Czechs 36, 38
D
Damascus 22, 22, 110
Danes 10
Dante Alighieri 89
Danube 10, 13
Deforestation 44–45
Denmark 32
Djenné 116
Dnieper 36, 37
Dome of the Rock 20
Domesday Book 99
Dominicans see Orders, Mendicant
Donations 61
Dragon, in Norse myth 9
Durham, Cathedral of 66
E
Education 82–83, 84
  monastic 84
  scholastic 84
Egypt 23, 115
El Cid Campeador (Rodrigo Diaz de Vivar) 104–105
Empire, Chinese 18–19, 20
Empire, Eastern Roman 7–8, 15–16, 22, 23, 29, 32, 33, 36, 37, 38, 38, 71, 75, 92, 106–108, 109, 118–119
Empire, Roman 4–8, 16, 24, 26, 30, 32
  agriculture 7
  army 7, 11
  economy 5, 7
  law 4, 16
  organization of society 5, 14
Empire, Western Roman 7–8, 20, 29, 42
England 79, 98–100, 102, 119
  Angle, Jute, and Saxon kingdoms 13
  civil wars 99
  Hundred Years' War 99, 102, 116
  Magna Carta 100, 100–101
  Norman Conquest 33
Ephesus 26
Epidemics 90–91, 91
Ethiopia, Empire of 115
Euclid 24
Europe
  economy and trade 41–42, 69, 74–80, 76, 89, 119

ethnic composition in the 9th century 10
  invasion by the Huns 12
  population 42, 68–69, 68, 69, 82, 90–91
F
Fairs 78–79, 79
Falconry 96–97
Famine 42, 91
Farmers, see Peasants
Fatimids 23, 115
Feudalism
  benefice 45, 46, 50, 52, 92, 93
  hereditary 48–49, 50
  economy 46–48, 50
  fief 48, 58, 93
  justice 48, 49, 54, 56
  organization of society 48, 49, 51-53, 58–61, 93, 98–99, 100, 103
Firearms 111, 116
Flagellants 91
Flanders 72–73, 76, 76, 79
Flora and fauna 40, 40–41, 43, 44–45, 56
Florence 69, 71, 74
  crafts 74
Fra' Dolcino 89
France 100–103, 102, 119
  English domination 99
  Hundred Years' War 99, 102, 116
  kingdom of 100–103
  Moorish settlements 30
Franchise 54, 56
Franciscans see Orders, Mendicant
Franks 8, 10, 13, 26–27
  army 26–27
  cavalry 27
  kingdom 26–27, 29
Fraxinetum 30
Frederick I Barbarossa 94, 96
Frederick II of Swabia 96–97, 96–97
G
Galen 24
Gallipoli 108
Gand 68, 76
Gaul 10, 13, 31
Genghis Khan 109, 110, 113
Genoa 71, 74, 75
Gepidae 11
Germans 8–11, 13–15, 32, 36
  agriculture 8, 11
  army 24

art *13*
Eastern 11
  myths *8–9*, 11
  organization of society 11
  religion 8, *12*, 14
  stock-raising 8
  weapons 11
Germany *79*, 98
  struggle between Church and
    Empire 94–96
Ghana, Kingdom of *115, 116*
Ghardaa *116, 117*
Gislebertus *65*
Gordian III, Roman emperor *17*
Gospel 87
Gothic *66*, 78, *84–85*, 84–86, *96*
  architecture 84–86
  cathedrals 84–86, *85*
  sculpture *85*
Greece
  art 4
  language 5, 15, 23, 96
  Roman occupation 16
Gregory IX, Pope *86*
Gregory VII, Pope 93
  Dictatus papae 94
  Gregorian Reform 93
Gunpowder 111
H
Han dynasty 19
Hanseatic League (Hansa) 76, *77*
Harold II 98
Harun ar-Rashid 23
Hastings, Battle of 98, *98–99*
Hellenism 4, 24
Henry VI 96
Henry II Plantagenet 99–100
Heresy *88–89*, 89–90, 102
Hinduism *18*
  Temple of Kharjauraho *18*
Hippocrates 24
Holy Land *51*, 53, 80, 83, 108
Holy Roman Empire 29–30, *29, 32*,
  33, 38, *38*, 39, 92, 94
  army 35
  organization of society 33
Horde 12
Horse
  in combat 11
  shoeing *35, 43*
Hospices 82
Hulagu Khan 110
Hungarians 31, 35, 38, 45
  religion 35, 36
  stock-raising 35

Hungary 35
Huns *10, 11*, 11–12, 15, 19, 35, 106
  organization of society 12
I
Iceland 33
Icon, Byzantine *107*
India 12, *18*, 19
Indian Gupta Empire *18*
Indo-Europeans 8–11
Ink *19*
Innocent III, Pope *87*, 90, 96
Inquisition *86, 88–89*, 90
Invasions *see also* Migrations
  barbarian 8, 80
  nomads of the steppes 111
  Turkish-Mongol 108–111
Investiture 51, *52, 92–93*, 93, 94,
  100
  investiture controversy *92*, 94
Islam 20–24, *20–22*, 31, *31*, 33, 71,
  80, *96*, 105, 108–110, 116,
  116–117 see also Muslims
  organization of society 108
  religion 20, *20, 21, 22*, 108
Ismaili sect *116*
Italy *39*, 80, 98
  at the time of Frederick II 97
  migrations of the Huns *11*
  Muslim bases 31, 32
  occupation by Ostrogoths and
    Lombards *10*
  struggle between Church and
    Empire 94, 96–97
  Ostrogoth kingdom 13
  Romanization of the barbarians
    13
J
Jaffa 75
Janissaries *108*
Japan *18*, 19
Jerusalem *20*, 26, *63*, 64
  Mosque of Omar *20*
  Temple of Solomon *20*
Jesters and entertainers *51*
Jesus 22, 80
Jews *81*
Joan of Arc, Saint *102*
John, King of England *101*
Journeymen 71
Jousts and tournaments *52–53*
Judaism 22
Julius Caesar 8
Jurchens 113
Justinian 16
Jutes *10*

K
Kaffa 75
Kaifeng 113
Kiev *34, 35*, 36, *37*, 77
Knights 50–53, *52-53*, 58, *80*, 82, *107*
  chivalry 52
  dubbing 51
  Templars *51*
Korea 20
Kublai Khan 110, 113
L
Lagny *79*
Landowners *see* Nobles
Languedoc 103
Latin Empire 108
Latin, language 5, 67, 96
Lechfeld, Battle of 38
Legnano, Battle of *94–95*
Leon-Castile, kingdom of 105
Liberal arts *82*
Loire 77, 103
Lombards *10*, 11
London 33, *69*, *98*
Lords and ladies 50, 46, 48 *see also*
  Nobles
Louis VI 102
Louis IX 103, *103*
Lübeck 76
Luni 33
M
Maghreb 116
Magna Carta 100, *100*
Mali, Kingdom of *114*, 116
Malines *68*
Mamluks 115
Manchuria 20
Manichaean sect 89
Maritime republics, Italian 74, 82
  trade 75, 82
Mathematics 24
Mecca *20, 21*
Medes, religion of 17
Medina *20*
Mediterranean
  architecture *13*
  culture and civilization *114*, 115
  Sea 4, *4*, *10*, 29, 33, 105, 118
  trade 71, 74–75, *77*
Mehmed II 118, *118*
Merchants *7*, 31, *63*, 71, 73, 74, 75,
  76–77, *77*, *78–79*, 79, 113–114,
  116, *116*
Merovingians 13, 27, 103
  art *13*
Meuse 77

Migrations 68, 92
    of central Asian nomads 12, 18
    of Germanic peoples 10–11, 12,
      13
    of the Huns 10–11, 12
    of the Slavs 10–11
Ming dynasty 114
Miramas-le-Vieux, fortress 30
Missi Dominici 29
Missionaries 29, 36
Monasteries 26–29, 31, 35, 43, 56,
      58, 60, 67, 68, 73, 83, 106
Monasticism 26–29
    cenobitic 26
    hermitic 26
    rise of 26
Money and coinage 46, 54, 71
Mongols 108, 108, 109–111, 118
    army 111
    cavalry 110, 111, 114
Monks 58, 67
Moors 30, 31, 31, 38, 104–105, 105
    see also Muslims
Moselle 77
Mossul 22
Muhammad 20, 20, 21, 22
Muslims 18, 26, 30, 31, 38, 80, 103,
      116 see also Islam
N
Nantes 33
Nara, 19
    Buddha 19
Navarre, kingdom of 105
Nibelungen 8, 9
Nicene Council 7
Nile 116
    Muslim centers 108
Nobles 35, 50–53, 54, 56, 61, 62, 73,
      74, 80, 82, 98, 98, 99, 100, 108
    dress 51
    food 50, 51
    homes 46–47, 49
Nomads 11–12, 18, 35, 36 see also
    Turks and Mongols
Normandy 98, 99, 107
    French domination 102
    Viking settlements 33
Normans 99 see also Vikings
Norman kingdoms 96–97, 97
Novgorod 34, 77
Nubia, kingdom of 116
O
Odin 8
Ogadai 110
Oleg 35

Orders, Mendicant 86–89, 86–87
    Dominicans 86, 87, 89
    Franciscans 86, 87, 87, 89
Orders, Monastic
    Benedictine 59, 60, 61
    Byzantine 106
    Cistercian 61, 61–62, 96
    Cluniac 59, 61–62
    of Mount Athos 106
Ostia 4, 5–7
Ostrogoths 10, 11
Otto I 38, 39, 93
Otto II 38
Ottoman Empire 108–109
Ottomans 108–109, 108
Ottonian Dynasty 38–39
P
Pagan religions 24, 37
Pagan temples 24
Palestine 80
Pannonia 35
Paper 18–19, 20
Paris 68, 69
    Abbey of Saint-Germain-des-
      Près 33
    Cathedral of Saint-Pierre-et-
      Saint-Paul 33
    Hungarian settlements 35
    Viking settlements 32
Parliament 100
Parthia, kingdom of 17
Patrimony of Saint Peter 97
Pavia 68
Pax Romana 5
Peasants 14, 43, 46, 53–56, 54–55,
      58, 68, 69, 82, 106
    food 55
    homes 44, 54–56
Pepin III the Short 27
Persia, Muslim centers 108
Persians 23
Perun 37
Philip I 100
Philip the Arabian 17
Philippe Augustus 102
Pilgrimages 21, 62–63, 62–65, 80
    armed 80, 80
Pilgrims 31, 62–65, 63, 64
    dress 63
    vesting ceremony 64
Pirates, Muslim 31–32
Pisa 33, 75
Plague 90–91, 91, 116
Plow 40–41, 43
Po River 77

Poems, epic 52, 104
Poitiers, Battle of 26
Poles 36
Polo, Marco 112–113
    The Travels of Marco Polo 112
Pope 26, 29, 35, 39, 60, 61, 62,
      88, 89, 92, 92–94, 97, 98,
      100, 107
Portugal, independence of 105
Portuguese people 118, 119
Preachers 87, 89
Printing 18–19, 113
Privilegium Othonis 39, 93
Provence 33, 80
Provins 79
Ptolemy 24
Q
Qangan 20
Qur'an 21
R
Reconquista 105
Renaissance 119
Renaissance, Carolingian 29–30
Revolution, agricultural 42–45, 54
Rheims, cathedral of 86
Rhine 29, 77
Rhone 77
    valley 35
Richard the Lion-Hearted 100
Roads see Communication routes
Roger II 97
Roman-Germanic
    art 12–13
    organization of society 14
Roman-Germanic kingdoms
      13–14, 16
Romanesque 65, 65–67, 66–67
    architecture 66–67
    churches 66–67, 67
    sculpture 64, 64–65, 67
Romans 4, 8, 10, 17, 20, 36, 40, 63
Rome 36, 64 see also Empire,
    Roman
    Biblioteca Vaticana 97
    decline of 7
    population in the Imperial Age 5
    population in the 11th century
      106
    port of 4–5
    Saint Peter's Basilica 38, 60
    Saracen invasions 30, 31
    trade 6
Rouen 33
Rus, Viking principality 34
Russia 33, 36, 111

Germanic settlements 11, 76, 76–77
Viking settlements 34–35
Russians 36
    religion 37
S
Saint Dominic (Domenico de Guzmán) 86, 89
Saint Peter 26
Saint James the Apostle 63
Saint Thomas à Becket, Archbishop of Canterbury 101
Saint Bernard de Clairvaux 62
Saint Francis of Assisi 87, 87
Saint Benedict of Norcia 24, 26, 29, 58
Saint-Lazare, church of 65
San Juan Bautista de Baños de Cerrato, Visigothic church of, 13
Sancho III the Great 105
Santiago de Compostela 62–63
    Saint James the Apostle, tomb of 62, 63, 64
Sardinia 31
Sasanid Empire 16, 16–18, 22, 23
Sasanids 17
    army 16–17
    cavalry 16, 17
    religion 17
    sculpture 17
Saxons 8, 10, 98
    religion 80
Saxony 29
Scandinavia 32, 76
Schola cantorum 58
Schools 83–84
    secondary 84
Scotti 10
Scriptorium 58, 59
Sects, heretic 89–90
Seigneurs, rural 14, 57, 62, 103 see also Nobles
Seine 32, 77
Seljuqs 107, 109
Serbians 36, 38
Serfs 53, 60, 62
Seville 33
Shapur I 17, 18
Ships
    carrack 74, 75
    Crusader 80, 81, 82
    flat-bottomed 77
    galleys 74, 75

Genoese 90
Ottoman 118
Roman 6
    sailing vessels 74
    transport ship 77
Vandal 10
Viking 32, 34
Shops and tradesmen 73, 87
Sicily 97
    Norman rule 96
    occupation by the Arabs 80
    occupation by the Saracens 31
Siegfried 8, 9
Slave trade 6, 22, 31, 35
Slaves 5, 6, 7, 14, 22
Slavs 35–38
    religion 36
Slovaks 36
Slovenes 36, 38
Song dynasty 110
Spain 80, 103–105
    culture 104
    influence of Islam 20
    Muslim settlements 26, 80
    occupation by Vandals 10
    Romanization of the barbarians 13
    Umayyad rule 23
    Visigoth rule 13
Spaniards 119
Spoleto, Church of Saint John and Paul 101
Stephan, king of Hungary 35
Stockholm 76
Strasbourg, cathedral of 86
Sudan, trade with Venice 75
Syria 17, 22
T
Tang dynasty 19, 20, 113
Tamerlane 110
Temmu, emperor of Japan 19
Thames 77
Thaumaturgy 102, 102–103
Theodosius 8
Theology 86
Theophano, princess 38
Thousand and One Arabian Nights, The 23
Tiber 4
Timbuktu 114–116, 116
Torture 89
Trade delegations 77
Trading companies 77
Trebizond 75

Trier 68
Troyes 78–79
    Cathedral of Saint-Pierre-et-Saint-Paul 78
Turks 36, 107, 108, 109, 110, 118
U
Ukrainians 36
Ulm, cathedral of 86
University 82–83, 84, 116
Urban II, Pope 80
V
Valdes (Peter Waldo) 89
Valencia, emirate of 104
Valerian 17, 18
Valhalla 8
Valkyries 8
Vandals 10, 11, 14
Vassallage 45–46, 93, 98
Vaults 66, 67, 85 see also Architecture
Venice 68, 74, 75, 81, 97 108
    Arsenal 74
    Biblioteca Marciana 89
    Gallerie dell'Accademia 75
    Republic of 97
    trade 75
Vikings 31, 32, 32–33, 38, 45
    art 35
    trade 32, 35
Villages and hamlets 45, 56, 56–57, 67, 69, 73 see also Cities
    Villafranca 56
    Villanova 56
Villani, Giovanni 97
    Cronica 97
Visigoths 8, 10, 103
Vistula 36
Vladimir, Prince 36, 37
W
Waldensians 89
Water-mill 40, 42
Weaving 72
William, Duke of Normandy 33
William I the Conqueror 98, 99
Wool processing 72, 73
Worms, Concordant of 94
Y
York 33
Ypres 76
Yüan dynasty 113, 114
Z
Zarathustra, doctrine of 17